# LOVE THY NEIGHBOR

This Large Print Book carries the
Seal of Approval of N.A.V.H.

# LOVE THY NEIGHBOR

## A MUSLIM DOCTOR'S STRUGGLE FOR HOME IN RURAL AMERICA

## AYAZ VIRJI

### *with Alan Eisenstock*

**THORNDIKE PRESS**
A part of Gale, a Cengage Company

Farmington Hills, Mich • San Francisco • New York • Waterville, Maine
Meriden, Conn • Mason, Ohio • Chicago

**LIBRARY OF CONGRESS CIP DATA ON FILE.
CATALOGUING IN PUBLICATION FOR THIS BOOK
IS AVAILABLE FROM THE LIBRARY OF CONGRESS**

ISBN-13: 978-1-4328-6557-3 (hardcover alk. paper)

Published in 2019 by arrangement with Convergent Books, an imprint of Random House, a division of Penguin Random House LLC

Printed in Mexico
1 2 3 4 5 6 7 23 22 21 20 19

*To Faisal, Imran, and Maya*

I begin in the name of God,
the most beneficent,
the most merciful.
If any good comes of this, then all
praises be to Him.
Only the mistakes belong to me.

# CONTENTS

# 1
## TOUGH QUESTIONS

2017.

A bitterly cold day in February.

I sit in the front row of the school auditorium as my friend Mandy France walks to the podium, tall, purposeful, the swell of her auburn hair flapping onto the shoulders of her pink blouse. My throat stings, on fire all day from a case of laryngitis. I cross and uncross my legs. I'm not nervous, exactly. Rather I feel jumpy, overeager, like a sprinter coiled in the starting blocks.

"Good evening," Mandy says to the audience.

Those two simple words calm me. Mandy has a way. A gift. Whenever I spend time with her, I feel bathed in warmth, softened by her humor. Her subtle spiritual power washes over and then lifts me. Especially lately.

"We're going to go ahead and get started," she says, the timbre of her voice sending out a signal. *Get ready. You need to hear this.*

On this chilly Thursday night in March, four hundred people — more than 25 percent of our town's population — have come to the school auditorium in Dawson, Minnesota, to hear a Muslim doctor speak about his faith. The doctor intends to tell the truth and enlighten people about Islam, a religion that has been repeatedly maligned and misrepresented in the media.

I am that doctor.

I am that Muslim.

Mandy holds for a slow two count and says, "I'd like to welcome you tonight to our presentation entitled 'Love Thy Neighbor.' For those of you who don't know me, I'm Mandy France, the current intern at Grace Lutheran here in Dawson. I am a fourth-year seminary student at Luther Seminary in St. Paul. I'll be graduating in May of this year with my master's of divinity degree and then going on towards ordination in the Evangelical Lutheran Church of America."

Translation:

*I am a Christian.*

Her credentials. Her passport. And in the town of Dawson — a rural community of fifteen hundred souls that nonetheless manages to keep five churches running — street cred. For a split second, I remember the night Mandy sat at our dining room table, telling a story that caused my wife, Musarrat, and me to laugh out loud. Some people from another church in town saw a yoga mat in Mandy's office and accused her of doing Islamic prayers in secret.

"As you all know, the rhetoric right now in our world surrounding the Muslim community is not the greatest," Mandy says. "It is hurtful, and the way the media has portrayed this community is harmful and it is wrong. That rhetoric has led to a lot of fear, something that is known as Islamophobia. For my internship project I decided to examine what it means to truly follow Jesus Christ's command to love thy neighbor."

Mandy turns to Musarrat and me and beams a contagious smile. My smile widens, mirroring hers.

She swivels away, looks straight ahead. Her forehead creases, and I catch a sudden look of determination.

"I knew Dr. Virji from the clinic and had visited him a few times, actually as my doctor. I knew his family was the only Muslim family living in this community, and I approached them and asked if they would share with me and the community about their faith."

She leans forward and speaks with insistence.

"They easily — *easily* — could have said no, but they graciously said yes and invited me into their home without hesitation. They both work fulltime jobs. They have three amazing children and took time out of their schedules to sit with me and educate me and answer my questions about their faith and talk about their experience being Muslim in America post 9/11."

Mandy shakes her head slightly. "These are people who are full of such grace, such dignity, and such acceptance of all people. To know this family is to know peace, and I can tell you that as a Christian person, I have learned more from them about what it means to follow the command 'Love thy neighbor' than I have from many Christians I have encountered in my life. I am honored to call them my friends and to call them my neighbors as well."

She takes a small step back to allow the words to sink in.

"Tonight, at this forum, we will have the opportunity at the end to engage in an open question-and-answer session. It is encouraged that you ask Dr. Virji those tough questions you have about the Islamic faith, the questions that you have about how the media portrays this faith, the questions you have wrestled with, the questions you might not otherwise ask. This is your chance to hear the truth from somebody who actually practices the faith."

I glance down at the outline I will use to deliver my speech, the eleven typed pages crinkling in my hands.

*Ask Dr. Virji those tough questions.*
*Questions you have wrestled with.*
*Questions you might not otherwise ask.*

Three years ago, when we moved to Dawson, and up until the election of Donald Trump, Musarrat and I never knew that our neighbors even *had* tough questions about us, questions they might be afraid to ask. We felt only acceptance and welcome. Since then I've wondered if those questions always existed and the election only brought them to the forefront.

I remember the first time we visited Dawson. We walked through the hospital where I would serve as chief of staff and head of the medical clinic. We toured the school our kids would attend. We strolled down the quaint main street, taking in the post office, barber shop, Wanda's Diner, the two-lane bowling alley, pharmacy, grocery store, the well-appointed library. Behind the main street, we saw an incongruous cluster of Victorian homes and approached the town park, where a quirky arrangement of garden gnome statues greeted us: Dawson's claim to fame, at least locally. Finally, most memorable of all, we met several warm, welcoming, down-to-earth people. Musarrat and I felt that we had found *home.*

"It's like a fairy tale," Musarrat, who wears a hijab, said. "No one stared at me."

But after Trump carried the county with close to 65 percent of the vote and Mandy began hearing from church members that people had questions — and concerns — about us, Musarrat said, "I knew there was something underlying. It was too good to be true."

I love Dawson. I love the small-town manners, the intimacy, the proximity of everything. I often walk to work, a welcome change from sitting in traffic on the way to every other job I've had. Our neighbors look out for us, drop in to say hi, shovel our sidewalk in the winter. We never lock our doors. We wouldn't think of it.

Dawson, too, was the place where my career became my calling. I left a high-end medical center in a midsize city because it practiced "turnstile medicine": *Move them in and out as fast as you can.* My position paid well, but that didn't matter. I felt frustrated and unfulfilled. In fact, I felt worse than that. I felt as if I wasn't doing what I had been trained to do, what I was *supposed* to do: provide attentive and complete medical care to people who would become my patients and stay my patients for a long period of time, maybe even their entire lives. Because I was on a clock, forced to attend to a certain number of patients per day, I found myself focusing only on Mr. Smith's chest pain and not on Mr. Smith. In order to practice what I call "dignified medicine," I would have to move.

Rural America was — and is — experiencing a severe doctor shortage. The latest statistics reveal a ratio of one doctor to 256 patients in cities compared with one doctor per 1,900 patients in rural America. So I convinced Musarrat to leave urban Pennsylvania, where we lived close to her family, and relocate to tiny Dawson, Minnesota, in farm country, at the far western tip of the state. As with any move, we experienced a period of adjustment and culture shock — we were the only Muslims in town — but by the end of the first year, we'd settled in. The kids found their stride in their new school. I hit the ground running at the hospital, adding six new service lines, upgrading the equipment, and helping oversee a multimillion-dollar hospital remodel and expansion. Musarrat opened what would soon become an in-demand skin care salon in the center of town. Clients came to her from all over, some from neighboring towns and others from as far as Minneapolis, three hours away.

Then — three years later — came the 2016 presidential election.

Reality hit us abruptly, harshly.

Our government turned cold, referring to Islam as a cancer and suggesting that Muslims be put on a registry.

Anti-Muslim sentiment and hate speech blew across the country like a wildfire.

Even in Dawson. Our family's home.

The day after the election I exploded with anger. I wanted to leave. To flee. To escape.

Then — soul-searching.

A calming. A call for justice. For explanation. For *truth.*

Resulting in this talk.

This necessary talk.

Mandy booked the Dawson-Boyd High School auditorium and put up flyers around town, announcing tonight's event. She used innocuous language, calling the talk simply "Love Thy Neighbor." The flyers explained that I would be speaking about my faith, about Islam.

Almost immediately, the phone calls started coming.

People expressed anger and outrage that the school would be hosting a "Muslim event." One hysterical person said she had heard that we intended to march children into a room, strap them into chairs, and force them to watch Muslim propaganda.

"That is the biggest fear I'm hearing," Mandy told me. "People think you are going to convert them."

"I don't know where that idea comes from," I said. "We don't have a call to spread the word. It's not our thing. It's kind of the opposite of our thing."

The phone calls and complaints continued. Someone accused Mandy of being a closet Muslim. Someone else called her a fake Christian. She phoned me in tears.

"I'm a Christian," she said. "I preach. I'm dedicating my life to preaching. I am a *Christian.*"

"I know," I said. "I'm so, so sorry this is happening to you."

"I will not be intimidated. We will do this talk, right?"

"Yes," I said. "We will."

Then, while she was visiting her family in Minneapolis, the superintendent of schools called and said he was concerned about the language she'd used in the flyers, specifically the word *Muslim.* Suppressing shock but wanting to calm the protests, Mandy agreed to pull all the advertising and rebrand the evening a "Christian-sponsored event."

But then the school board called to discuss our request to live stream the event. We'd rented the auditorium and believed that we would have access to the school's audiovisual equipment. Not only did the members of the school board refuse to give us AV equipment to record the event, they asked Mandy for additional funds to rent the facility for the evening.

"You want more money?" Mandy asked. "Why? I don't understand."

"We think you should pay for our time," a member of the school board said. "We have spent so many extra hours discussing this. We've had parents calling, we've had to arrange for additional meetings."

"Above and beyond," someone else said.

Mandy lost it. "You know that Dr. Virji is the chief of staff of the hospital and the director of the medical clinic, right? He's one of the most respected people in this community. Everybody knows him. Musarrat runs one of the most outstanding businesses in town. Everybody knows *her*. People drive from everywhere to see these two. This is who you're dealing with. This is who they're protesting."

In the end we paid the extra money, gave up on live streaming, and rented our own audiovisual equipment. We had committed to this evening, no matter what. Nothing would deter us.

"So," Pastor Mandy says, focusing on the audience before her, "tonight there will be guidelines as we engage in this conversation between two faiths. First, I ask that you speak out of your own experience. Please do not speak on behalf of an entire community. Use 'I' statements when you ask a question. Do not assume that all people think the way you do."

Then she goes right to the heart of the protestors' biggest fear.

"We are not here to *convert,*" she says. "We are not here even to come to an agreement. We are here to understand and to learn to build bridges because in our society we build far too many walls."

It's a direct reference to the election, to the rhetoric that cuts me. *Separate them. Isolate them. Remove them. Build. A. Wall.*

"You are encouraged to challenge ideas," Mandy says, "but it will not be tolerated if

21

you personally attack. If you choose to use words that could be interpreted as harmful or hateful, you will be asked to leave. This forum is entitled 'Love Thy Neighbor,' and we are not here to make others feel anything less than loved."

I'm not surprised at her directness, but I look around the room and wonder who will carry out her mandate. I don't see any extra security or police. I'm not exactly sure who would come forward to remove any protestors or hate speakers.

"With that being said," Mandy says, speaking now with a fervor I didn't expect and words that humble me, "it is with the utmost pleasure and joy that I introduce you to our guest of honor and some of the most brilliant and amazing people that I have ever had the honor of meeting and talking with: Dr. Ayaz Virji, his amazing wife, Musarrat, and their children, Faisal, Imran, and Maya. Please give them a round of applause."

I stand, smile at my family, and climb the stairs to the stage. At the podium, I place my outline and water bottle in front of me and look out into a bank of surprisingly blinding lights. I squint, searching for Musarrat's face.

Only then do I hear the audience applauding, a sudden, rocking wave that builds into a standing ovation. I can't see the people in the audience, but I can *feel* them. The heat of their collective embrace vibrates through me.

"Thank you, everyone," I say as the applause subsides. "Thank you for that very kind welcome."

The audience sits and goes quiet, and I continue to squint into the glare of the lights. I briefly shield my eyes with my hand.

"It's so great to see so many of you here," I say with a rasp in my voice. I saw back-to-back patients today and whispered to all of them in order to save my voice for this hour-long talk. I'll need to pace myself and sip water to get through it.

"So I want to say first and foremost, thank you to Pastor Mandy and to Grace Lutheran Church. I will tell you it has been an honor to meet her, her husband, Pastor Kelly, and her daughter."

I lower my voice, trusting the microphone to pick up what I will say next, a thought that, to me, suddenly seems the most crucially important words I will say.

"I need to remind all of you — and myself — that I wasn't the one who initiated this. It was Grace Lutheran who came to me and asked me to speak, to help dispel myths."

I swallow and pause. I want to choose my next words extremely carefully.

"My . . . faith . . . is very personal. I don't go around talking about it. But the . . . *feeling* in society and the *context* has come to a point where a talk like this is needed. It's only through inspiration from people like Pastor Mandy, whom I learn from, that I come here and hopefully give you some information that may be of benefit to all of us. And hopefully, maybe we can start a dialogue based on truths, not on media, not on sensationalism."

My voice cracks as it rises. "I want to talk from love and humanity and diversity. These are the premises of your faith. You know that very well. These are the premises of my faith. These are the premises of *every* faith."

I look down at my outline. I'm lost. I've spoken from my heart, but what I've just said comes from an entirely different place in my outline. I realize it doesn't matter. I've found a new place. My place is here, in this moment. I close my eyes and recite the Islamic phrase I say before I pray.

"I begin in the name of God, the most beneficent and most merciful. If any good comes out of this talk, then all praise goes to Him. Only the mistakes belong to me."

I open my eyes, hold for a beat to take in

24

the silence in the auditorium, and say, "First I want to introduce myself. Many of you know me. I am a physician. I work here in Dawson. I have been here about three years. We absolutely love the people in Dawson. It has been a pleasure to live in this community and to meet so many sincere people, people who speak honestly, from their hearts. Coming here to rural America — which is brand new for us — I have seen, in so many people, a dignified and humane way to approach life. We talk about this stuff all the time. It is a gem to be around you. We have had so many people thank us for being here. We want to thank you for allowing us to be here."

Then something strange happens. I become aware of a kind of electrical current pulsing through the audience. Somewhere beneath the other, random sounds that surround it — a mash-up of bodies rustling, feet shifting, throats clearing, voices murmuring — there is a thrumming pulse that seems to show me my *purpose.* My need to be here. To talk to these people and connect with them. I can't make out any of the four hundred faces in front of me, but — that *pulse . . .*

I'm feeling the beating of their hearts.

I swallow, my voice scratchy.

"So." I press the soles of my feet into the stage floor and cement myself *here,* in the present. I need this audience, all of them Christians, to know that I understand them, at least to some degree — more than they understand me — and so I say, smiling, "I want to tell you . . . I went to a Lutheran school for ten years of my life, from pre-K to tenth grade."

I exhale softly and say, "I have very good memories of that time. I went to church just like many of you do. I didn't know Islam at the time." There it is.

My confession. My revelation.

"I went to a Catholic institution after high school — Georgetown University — for undergrad and medical school. I was very humbled by the intellect and scholarship among the Jesuits and the Catholics. I took classes at the Center for Muslim-Christian Understanding, and I was blown away. John Voll, who is a Protestant, was one of my favorite professors at Georgetown. I'm very, very thankful to him. He taught me of the writings of St. Thomas Aquinas and introduced me to so much more. Amazing stuff. I learned a great deal about Christianity. I continue to study other religions in my spare time. Christianity is a religion of love, of kindness, of peace, of justice. I am very proud and happy to have gone to Christian schools. It was my honor to do so."

I pause and hear — silence. No one stirs. My throat raw, my thoughts careening, I say, "We can't be scared of each other. We need to join together and build a foundation of love and respect. We don't have to agree with everything, but let's know first. I would hope we can do that. Let's *know.*"

I suddenly feel unsteady. I squeeze my eyelids shut and grip the sides of the podium. For the briefest moment, I feel myself drifting off into a memory. I am not here. I am in a different time, a different place . . .

I see a highway . . . a white sun . . .

Clearwater, Florida.
2003.
Two years after 9/11.

A young woman, twenty-three, a cautious yet confident driver, checks the rearview mirror of her van and glances over her right shoulder at her two children, aged nine months and two years old, strapped in their car seats behind her. She smiles at them, turns back, lightens her grip on the steering wheel, and absently pats her hijab, her head scarf. She drums her fingertips on the steering wheel and again checks the rearview mirror.

That's when she sees the Jeep. It roars up to her rear bumper, nearly smashing into it, then swerves into the right-hand lane and pulls alongside her. She doesn't want to make eye contact with the driver, but she catches a glimpse of him in her peripheral vision. His features blur. All she knows for sure is that he is white.

The driver shoves his head out of his window and screams an obscenity at the young woman. She recoils, blinks, her mouth quivering. She sees that he is clutching a baseball bat. He waves it at her like a weapon, waggling it, and then he swings it toward her car.

The young woman gasps. Tears leak down her face. She leans forward and steps on the accelerator.

The driver of the Jeep speeds up, keeping pace. Suddenly he whips his steering wheel sharply, and the Jeep crosses into her lane.

"Go *home!*" the driver of the Jeep screams.

*I am home,* the young woman says to herself, tears pooling in her eyes. *This is my home.*

The Jeep swerves out of her lane and then back, the driver laughing now, waving the bat, taunting her, pretending to be about to ram the Jeep into the side of her van. Feeling trapped, the young woman grips the steering wheel, her fingers turning chalk white.

"Mommy!" she hears from the back seat.

"It's okay," she says, her voice trembling. "Everything's fine."

Ahead, a traffic light flashes from yellow to red. For a second, the young woman considers running the light, but she thinks of her two children in the back seat and steps on the brake.

"Please," she whispers, a prayer through her tears.

Just that — *please.*

No other words come.

The driver of the Jeep pulls up next to her and leans half of his body out the window. He curses at her again, thrusts the bat toward her car. And then, as if God has answered the young woman's one-word prayer, the Jeep speeds down a nearby exit ramp and disappears.

The traffic light turns green. The young woman, frozen, her mind blank, her heart hammering, finally becomes aware of car horns bleating behind her. She sniffs, eases the van slowly forward, and drives three more miles to her destination, the doctor's office.

She enters the medical building with her

baby in her arms and her two-year-old's hand clasped in hers. She charges past the receptionist and pushes into the doctor's office, startling the doctor, a young man of twenty-nine.

I am the doctor. The young woman is my wife.

I leap up from behind my desk, take our baby, Imran, cradle him against my chest, and hold Faisal's small hand.

Only then does Musarrat allow herself to let go. The sobs come in force, achingly, nearly driving her to her knees.

"Ayaz," she wails. *Where are we?*

I blink the memory away. Peering into the audience, I realize that my eyes have become accustomed to the glare of the lights. I pick out Musarrat among the tide of shimmering faces, remembering how she didn't wear her head scarf for several years after that incident on the highway, until we moved out of Florida.

I take a deep breath and look down at my outline.

"I heard there were many people who were protesting this talk," I say. "Obviously, that stings a little bit. Of course you have the right to protest. You have the right to call the superintendent or the police department or whatever and talk about your fears. But . . . this is not a conversion fest. I have zero interest in that. My advice, from my heart, to any Christian, would be that you should love like Jesus, pray like Jesus, and live like Jesus. If you do that, you will be better than ninety-nine percent of all people in the entire world — *including Muslims.*"

I swallow, pause, and then whisper into the microphone, my voice echoing through the silent auditorium.

"I understand that some people felt threatened. I hope you don't. I know it's not the majority. I know it's a small minority. I know that."

I stab my finger at the outline and read, "From Proverbs: 'Never rely on what you think you know. Never let yourself think you are wiser than you are. The Lord corrects the ones He loves. Wisdom is more valuable than jewels. The Lord created the earth by His wisdom.' And Muhammad said, 'The ink of a scholar is holier than the blood of a martyr.' "

I pause and then say, "I know that for some of you, this is the first time you've ever heard from the 99.99 percent of Muslims. There are 1.7 billion Muslims in the world. According to the State Department, two hundred thousand, at most, are labeled as terrorists. That comes out to 0.01 percent. What you see in the far-right media — that's not us. That 0.01 percent are insane. They are a disgrace to my religion. They are a disgrace to me. They are a disgrace to humanity. I condemn them. They pervert my religion. They have nothing to do with Islam. They are splinter groups. It's like saying that Christianity is the KKK or David Koresh and Heaven's Gate and the Jonestown massacre or the Salem witch trials. That would be a distortion of your religion. It would be very disingenuous of me to do that because Jesus was a man of peace. In my opinion, those people are not Christians. They don't represent Christianity."

I catch my breath, and when I speak next, my voice rises. "All I'm saying is please, when it comes to other religions — to my religion — let's know the facts. There's no such thing as *alternative* facts. There are either facts or falsehoods. Truth or lies. Let's not judge without knowing. Is that not sensible? Is that not the right way? To all of those people who protested this talk, I ask them — I ask you —"

Behind me, my face appears projected on a screen. I'm wearing a lab coat, a tie, and a wide smile. I look so young, almost like a kid playing doctor. I shrug at the audience.

32

"Do I look that intimidating?"

The silence in the auditorium burns through me.

"Do I look like a terrorist?"

# 2
## WHERE AM I?

Twenty-one years ago.

Washington, DC.

I am a third-year medical student at Georgetown. I walk through each day wasted, exhausted, stumbling forward on fumes. We are, all of us, med students. Human husks surviving on junk food and sense memory, jumping at the beck and call of our residents and interns. The attending surgeons assign us "scut" work, loosely defined as the most menial, boring, mind-numbing jobs on the agenda, considered beneath any real doctor. The term, I believe, had its derivation in the early 1900s, referring to the lowest scullery work performed in ships' kitchens: peeling potatoes, scrubbing pots and pans, dumping out trash.

As third-year med students, we spend the year moving among different rotations, with the goal of introducing us to all the possible specializations and identifying which one fits us best. In other words, we are determining what kind of doctor we want to be.

In our rotations, we shadow attending doctors and learn mostly by observing. We do whatever the attendings ask, whenever they ask it. We ask no questions. We offer no suggestions. We just do what they say and say nothing ourselves. On rare occasions we assist during a medical procedure. More often we take medical histories, type up forms, and do rounds on patients — checking on them and writing a report — often at night while the rest of the world sleeps. On certain days, usually at the end of a brutal sleepless shift, I feel less like a doctor and more like a zombie.

One morning, during my orthopedic surgery rotation, I attend to a patient, a young woman, stricken with a bad melanoma. The cancer has eaten into her face, boring all the way down to the bone. She will need extensive orthopedic surgery. Dr. K, my attending surgeon, has asked me to do the young woman's preoperative physical and medical history, which essentially involves taking her blood pressure and asking a series of routine questions. Scut work.

I arrive at the young woman's room, clipboard in hand, stethoscope and hospital credentials draped around my neck. I knock gently on the door and step into the room.

"Hi," I say, moving to the young woman's bedside. "I'm Ayaz Virji, your student doctor. I'm going to do your physical and take your history."

The patient nods and begins lifting herself by her elbows to a sitting position in her bed.

That's when I notice him.

Sitting in a chair in the corner.

A young man her age, her boyfriend, I assume, leans heavily forward, his legs spread wide, jeans tucked into cowboy boots. His massive forearms rest on bulky thighs, and his chest strains the seams of a plaid shirt. A quick glance tells me that he's carrying three hundred pounds at least, and I calculate that he stands well over six feet tall. He wears a neatly trimmed jet-black mustache that accentuates the paleness of his skin. He stares at me with blank, steely blue eyes.

I turn away, take a seat next to the patient, and focus on her. I've learned, first as an undergrad and then as a med student, to employ a kind of tunnel vision, concentrating completely on the task at hand.

"How are you doing?" I ask her.

She shrugs.

"I know," I say. "I hear you. Well, this will only take a few minutes."

Behind me, out of my sight line, the boyfriend clears his throat and shifts his considerable weight.

"Let's start with your history," I say to the young woman. "These are all very standard questions. Okay. Do you have any allergies?"

The woman murmurs a low "No," and I note her response on the sheet attached to my clipboard.

"Have you had any past surgical complications?"

Another muted "No."

Then I feel a sudden — chill. It's as if a bitter, jagged wind has blown into the room and knifed into my spine. I shiver. I stare at my clipboard. I want to race through the questions and get out of here.

"Have you had problems with any anesthesia?"

"No."

"Are you allergic to any medication?"

"No."

"Are you feeling well today?"

A chair scrapes the floor, and a presence fills the room. I lift my eyes from the patient and see her boyfriend cross the room in what seems like two steps. He pulls up a foot away, his immense size looming over me. I stand, practically jumping out of my chair. The top of my head barely reaches his chin.

"What is your position in her surgery?" he asks. "I —"

I swallow once, twice, realizing that I have momentarily lost the ability to speak. Whatever else I have to say has become lodged in my throat. I swallow again, and somehow the words dislodge and rise to my lips, and I speak more rapidly than I ever have in my life. "I . . . am a *student* . . . and I will be in the operating room. Basically, we assist the attending surgeons. It might be to hold an instrument or help to retract or, I don't know, we just do whatever the surgeons ask. Sometimes we just observe."

The boyfriend dips his head and reads my name badge.

"Virji," he says, dragging out both syllables, taking what feels like thirty seconds to pronounce my name.

He raises his eyes from my name badge and scowls.

And then he walks into me.

I back up.

He keeps walking.

I back into the corner and reach my hands behind me so I can feel the wall. The boyfriend keeps walking. He stops two inches away from me, shoving his massive body forward. I smell his musky aftershave and cigarette smoke on his breath.

"You will not have anything to do with her procedure," he says.

My palms begin to sweat.

"You understand that?"

I nod. My entire body begins to shake.

"If you do, I will find you."

He once again stares at my name badge. He pronounces my name again, this time spitting both syllables into my face.

My hands trembling, my voice quivering, I say, "I will make my attending surgeon aware of your concerns."

Then — I have no idea how — I duck and wriggle away from him. Clutching my clipboard, I sprint out of the hospital room.

I run to the end of the hall, spin around the first corner I come to, and press against the wall to catch my breath. I look down at my hands. They are shaking violently. I study my sweaty palms, close my eyes, and whisper a prayer. After staying locked against the wall for what feels like five full minutes, my heart rate and breathing return to normal. Feeling slightly light-headed, I walk down the hallway to Dr. K's empty office and wait for him.

When he comes in twenty minutes later, I pace the room and tell him what happened with the boyfriend. The words barrel out of my mouth in one breathless, nonstop sentence.

"I'm still shaking, Mike." I look at him, my eyes starting to tear. "Listen, man, I don't think I should be in on this procedure."

"You can't let that guy get to you. You have to be in on the procedure. It's part of the learning process."

"Please, Mike, no. Please don't make me go in."

Dr. K leans forward in his chair, taps his pen on his desk, and looks at me. "Okay," he says. "You can stay outside."

My stomach literally unclenches in relief. "Thank you," I say.

Word travels. Residents and med students come to me, offering outrage, encouragement, support, and sympathy, all expressing variations of "Don't worry about that guy."

Even though I feel buoyed by everyone's support, I still refuse to go into the operating room. I stay completely out of the procedure. I play no part in it. I don't make an appearance. I have absolutely nothing to do with it.

I can't change any other part of my schedule, though, and that night I make the rounds of the postoperative patients with

Dr. K. As we go from room to room, a sense of dread begins to seep into me. Before long, we arrive outside the young woman's room. I freeze at the door. I cannot move.

"Come on," Dr. K says. "You have to go in there."

"I can't. Let me stay out in the hall. Please."

"You have to come in, Ayaz," Dr. K says. "Don't worry. I'll do all the talking. You're just going to hang back and observe."

"I really, really don't think I should —"

"I know. But you have to."

My mouth goes dry. Before I can say another word, Mike strides into the room. I follow behind him, imagining that I can somehow disappear into the flaps of his blue scrubs. I scan the room frantically, and then I see the boyfriend sitting in the corner.

He glares at me, grunts, and slowly gets to his feet.

I lower my head. I don't dare make eye contact.

"Hey, there," Mike says, moving to the patient's side and taking her hand to check her pulse.

I keep my eyes pinned to the floor.

"How you doing?" Mike asks, looking at her face and nodding at the bandages.

"I'm doing fine," she says.

I try to swallow but can't. My mouth feels as though it has filled with sand.

"I've checked your chart," Mike says to the patient. "Everything's going along the way it should. So okay, terrific. We'll see you later."

He nods at me. I turn to follow, but I can't move. My feet feel cemented to the floor. I take one step, and my knees begin to tremble. I fight through it and walk slowly behind Mike, my head still down, aiming blindly toward the door. When I look up, the door suddenly appears minuscule and the length of a football field away.

I force myself to move toward it — slowly — painfully.

I reach for the doorknob —

"DOCTOR."

The boyfriend. His voice reverberates through the room.

"I need to talk to you."

My spine goes cold.

The boyfriend moves on a straight line toward Mike. I take a long step to the side, giving him as wide a path as I can.

*I want to disappear,* I think. *I want to melt into the floor.*

Then, in my peripheral vision, I see the boyfriend's index finger stabbing the air in my direction.

"I don't know what the hell is wrong with this guy," he says, his finger pointing at me like a blade. "I don't know if he has a racial problem or what have you."

My jaw drops. I look up, my lips quivering.

*Me? I'm the one with the racial problem?*

"You know what I told him?" the boyfriend shouts, his finger still pointed at me. "I told him that I *did not want him involved at all in my girlfriend's care.*"

Then he threatens me.

I don't remember his exact words. I don't *hear* the exact words. But I don't need to hear them to remember the violence that spewed from him. I hear the hate.

The silence that follows seems like forever.

Finally, Mike says, softly, "Okay, we will take what you're saying under advisement. Just for your information, Dr. Virji was not involved in the procedure. He is assisting me, but he was not in the operating room."

We leave the room. The moment we hit the hallway, my eyes begin to water.

I shake my head. "Mike —"

"This is unacceptable," he says. "He threatened you. We're filing a police report tomorrow morning."

That night I go home hoping to catch two or three hours' sleep before I have to return

43

to the hospital for early rounds. I arrive at our apartment, feeling numb, my hands still shaking. I enter the small living room and slump onto our couch, trying to settle myself and not wake Musarrat, my young wife. After a moment, I scoot to the edge of the couch, survey the room, and — impulsively, irrationally — search for something to protect myself and Musarrat. I have no familiarity with weapons. I have never fired a gun and would not know where to get one. We have a few sharp knives, one with a serrated edge that we use to cut bread and tomatoes. But even that feels equally inadequate and ridiculous. My mind turns to the baseball bat that we keep in the closet. I spring off the couch, grab the bat, carry it into the bedroom, and place it under the bed. As I undress, I see that Musarrat is wide awake and looking at me strangely.

"Why did you just put the baseball bat under the bed?"

I don't want to worry her, but I can't help myself. My feelings are too raw, too close to the surface.

"During rounds, this guy threatened me," I say. "A patient's boyfriend."

Musarrat sits up in the bed. "Why?"

"Because I have brown skin."

"Ayaz —"

"I'm serious. Do not open the door to anybody except me. The guy is scary. We're going to file a police report."

I sit on the bed and rest my head in my hands. After a moment, I feel my wife's hands gently kneading my back. For the first time in what seems like twenty-four straight hours, the tension in my body starts to release.

"Sometimes —" I say, too emotionally and mentally drained to complete the thought.

"I know," Musarrat says. "I know."

The next morning I'm swamped. After a fitful night of sleeping off and on for maybe three hours, I go to the hospital for early rounds. Then I have grand rounds, a kind of classroom lecture during which I'm required to wear a shirt and tie and present to our attending doctor, Dr. Delahay, a tough, no-nonsense surgeon whom I thoroughly admire. After grand rounds, I change out of my shirt and tie and into my scrubs to assist on a surgery.

Somehow — between early rounds, grand rounds, and the surgery — I go to the hospital security office and file a report. After I leave, a security guard locates the boyfriend in the patient's room and attempts to talk to him. The guy goes berserk, and the security guard calls in the DC

45

police, who take him to the local police station. At the end of the day, the police officers return the boyfriend to hospital security and isolate him on a vacant floor in the hospital. The security guards issue him an official warning. They tell him they are going to kick him and his girlfriend out of the hospital.

The guy backs down.

Not only does he back down, he appears contrite, apologetic.

Hospital security and then Dr. Delahay and Dr. K contact me. They suggest I go through something called a resolution procedure.

"What do I have to do?" I ask.

"Pretty much what it sounds like," Dr. Delahay says. "You sit down with the guy and resolve your differences."

"I don't have any differences," I say. "He threatened me."

"The idea is that he will apologize to you."

"You mean he will be *forced* to apologize to me."

"Something like that, yeah."

As I consider the idea, the trembling returns to my knees.

"I really don't want to do that," I say. "I don't want to be in a room with this guy. I don't want to see his face ever again. Twice before was more than enough."

"I wasn't asking," Dr. Delahay says.

I suddenly feel heartsick and deeply, truly afraid. Those emotions must be apparent, because Dr. K says quietly, "I'll go with you."

We arrive at a virtually uninhabited floor of the hospital and enter a room. The boyfriend stands at the far end, his mustache neatly trimmed, his hair combed back and glistening with gel, his white face flushed. Two burly security guards greet Dr. K and me, and then they nod at the boyfriend. He walks toward us. He passes me and faces Mike, avoiding me completely.

"Listen," he says, his head bobbing, never — not once — looking directly at me. "I didn't mean anything by, you know, *anything.* I'm sure he's a fine young man — as I am a fine young man. This was definitely a problem of miscommunication. I am not a violent person. I had no intention of doing anything, you know, violent, or hurtful, or whatever. Nothing like that."

I want to scream —

*That's no apology!*

*You're a racist. An unapologetic racist.*

But the guy will not look at me. He keeps his eyes locked on Mike.

Then something inside me clicks, a switch

turning on or turning off, I can't be sure. I can't even define what I feel. I just — *feel* it. A change.

Until now I have felt as though I am a victim, as though being brown and a Muslim were somehow *less than.* I have been bullied and diminished, and I have reached the end of my rope. But now my nerves, so recently shattered, settle and calm. I no longer feel anything but strength and certainty. And I begin to put a name to that change, that click. Call it awareness. No — call it *love.* Of who I am.

I'm done cowering to this guy and to people like him, from this point on until forever. I am a doctor — and I have had enough. I draw myself up to my full height and stare this guy — this racist — right in the eye.

"I have to go," I say. "I'm on call."

A tremor moves through my body as I think about that incident. Then I remember —

Four years ago.

I am a doctor. I work at a medical center in suburban Pennsylvania. We administer to a high volume of patients, our directive to move people in and out as fast as is reasonably possible. Turnstile medicine. I have decided to leave the practice. I am changing my lifestyle and my life. I am moving to a medical clinic and hospital in tiny Dawson, Minnesota. I want to give more time and attention to my patients — all the time they need. I want to offer what we call dignified medicine. This decision came about through hours and hours of soul-searching and prayer, asking myself —

*Where am I? What is my center?*

Eventually I find it.

My center, my drive, becomes defined by one motivation.

To do the right thing.

Which is not easy, because the right thing may not be the obvious thing.

You have to search for it, discover it, embrace it. And when you make the commitment to do the right thing, you often discover that doing the right thing is hard.

*Change your life. Go to rural America. Be a doctor there. Serve. You will be alone. But you have to go because you're needed.*

It's hard.

When I think about how I want to live my life, I realize I'm driven toward one goal: to try to leave the world a little bit better. The goal feels intimidating and huge and often unattainable. But I can't let that stop me. Even when an event like the one that follows foreshadows what I may face as the only Muslim in a community of white Anglo-Saxon Protestants.

I still have a few weeks left in Pennsylvania, so I continue moving patients in and out of that revolving door. Sometimes I drift away in my mind, imagining myself in small-town Dawson, practicing dignified medicine, attempting to become the doctor that I am determined to be. I go to this secret place in my mind at night while Musarrat and I pack and make final arrangements for our move. But by day I am *here,* in this practice, in Pennsylvania. I am able, thankfully, to focus, to be present. And then one afternoon, pushing the door open as I read the patient's chart, I see that I will be examining a middle-aged woman with a history of high cholesterol. I put down the chart and smile at my patient. She is wearing a gown and sitting on the examination table. She squirms as I approach her.

That's when I notice her fingernails — chipped, gnarled, curling, twisted beyond what would seem humanly possible, each one the size of a small finger.

"My God," I say. "Your nails."

I extend my hands toward hers. She flinches, hesitates, then spreads her hands. I can't help but gawk. The nails are nine inches long.

"I've never cut them," she says.

She speaks with a mixture of pride and rebellion.

"I can see that," I say. "But why not?"

She withdraws her hands and places them palms down on the examination table.

"Because Jesus hasn't told me to," she says.

I back up and snatch her chart. I glance at her personal information — address, age, occupation. She has a home, a good job, no indication of mental illness. She seems — normal. Except for the disturbing Cruella de Vil fingernails.

I put her chart into its sleeve on the back of the door and study her nails for a solid twenty seconds.

"You've got really bad fungi in those nails," I say. "They look infected."

I wait for a response. She stares ahead, avoiding my eyes.

"That infection could spread," I offer. "It can go into other areas of your body."

She says nothing. She looks past me.

"It's very dangerous," I say. "You really need to trim your nails —"

She stares into me.

"I will," she says. "When Jesus tells me to."

■ ■ ■ ■

I look out into the auditorium, the hot, bright lights causing the faces of the audience in front of me to shimmer. I see pale shapes, forms, but I cannot make out any human features.

*An audience of ghosts,* I think.

I close my eyes now and drop my voice. "One hour of introspection — sitting, thinking, reflecting. I do this all the time. I do it multiple times throughout the day. I say, 'Who am I? Why am I here? Where am I going?' "

I open my eyes. The glare of the lights burns.

"Who am I?" I repeat. "I am a caretaker. I am a caretaker of my family, of those around me, of my patients. I am a caretaker of all God's creations. All of them."

I remember the first night we came to Dawson —

I steer the rental car along Route 212, a two-lane highway that runs from Minneapolis to Dawson, a straight shot, the GPS promises. We drive through farmland and over rolling hills, past farmhouses and silos. The sky is so wide and expansive that it seems to touch the grass. In my peripheral vision, I see Musarrat and the kids peering out their windows, practically gawking at the wide-open spaces as dusk settles. It feels as if I'm driving into a blank slate. I embrace the image, and a feeling of calm descends.

Out here in the far corner of the Midwest, night falls hard. All of a sudden, we are driving into darkness. It simply descends. We have no streetlights to illuminate us and poor or no signage to guide us. It feels like a different country, unmarked territory. Finally, even the GPS gives up. I slow down as we drive though a cluster of four or five stores and then realize that we've just gone through an entire town.

Ten minutes later, we pass through a similar town, another six-store main street. Then, fifteen minutes later, another town, this one larger because it has a stoplight.

Time clicks by, and the hour gets later. A sense of unease worms into my stomach.

*Minneapolis to Dawson — a straight shot,* I remind myself. *Can't miss it.*

Somehow we do.

We overshoot it.

We drive right through it, I guess.

Then I definitely take a wrong turn — because I leave Route 212, turn down a barely visible gravel road, and drive a

53

quarter mile or so into the mouth of blackness. I slow the car to a crawl and then stop.

After twenty seconds of tense silence, Musarrat says, "This isn't right."

"I know," I say, trying to appear calm.

"Are we lost?" one of the kids asks from the back seat.

"No," I say. "We just took a wrong turn. We're not lost."

*Oh, we're lost.*

I glance at the clock on the dash. It reads 12:03 a.m. We're into tomorrow.

"We have to turn — around," I say.

"Yes," Musarrat says. "That would be a good idea."

*I'm a cliché,* I think. Your typical male, hopelessly lost, attempting to appear in charge and competent. Pretending — until a few moments ago — that I know the way. At this point, midnight in the middle of nowhere, I would not be too proud to ask anyone. Although, squinting into this eerie barren blackness, maybe I wouldn't.

I admit it.

I'm scared. But I don't want Musarrat to see that my left leg is pumping and my palms are dripping with sweat.

I can't admit my fear because I feel a powerful responsibility for the four other humans in this car.

It was my idea to come here. This was my choice, my decision. This is on me.

I honestly don't remember much of what happened next.

I turn the car around, tires crunching on gravel, creating a loud, jarring sound that thankfully muffles the pounding of my heart. Somehow we find our way out.

I ease onto the highway and head the opposite way on Route 212 . . . I think . . . I'm pretty sure. I honestly don't know. But after a few minutes, I recognize a gas station we passed before, a bend in the road, a familiar nondescript building, a fast-food place, and then, miraculously, we arrive at the area's one and only hotel, where we have a reservation. After the frenzy of signing the guest log, checking in, lugging suitcases, and opening doors, I find myself lying in bed, wide awake, my clothes on, my heart pounding, my pulse raging, my hands shaking, a whirlwind of thoughts crashing through my brain —

Why did I uproot my family for — *this*?

What if this doesn't work out?

What if I've made a huge mistake?

We had a comfortable life, why did I have to change everything?

What have I *done*?

*Where am I?*

# 3
## DIGNIFIED MEDICINE

I think about my daily prayers, all the reflection, introspection, and outright asking for guidance and strength as I embarked on this new phase of life. My journey. I do believe that this move grew out of ethical conviction, a drive to help people in rural America. I felt as strongly about that as I had when I helped create a free clinic in DC during medical school. I believe I have always been on a journey, a search for the right path.

My father, too, was a searcher, a man constantly on the move.

I think of his struggle, of how hard he and my mother worked to make a life for their young family. I'm sure that it is from my father that I inherited my relentless drive and energy, even, some might say, restlessness. I am always in motion.

I am of Indian descent, born in Mombasa, Kenya, a coastal city, the second largest in the country. Soon after I was born, my mother, father, and two older brothers moved to the United States. They left me behind with my grandparents for six months, and the three of us joined my parents after they settled in Florida. I have no memory of my infancy in Mombasa. I remember only Florida.

"Are you from India?" I have been asked.

"No, I'm from *Florida*," I say, sometimes with an intended edge.

Neither of my parents went to college, both of them graduating only from high school. My father, especially, was very driven, very industrious. He and my mother traveled all over the world, from the slums of Zanzibar all the way through Europe. They settled briefly in Italy, where my mother gave birth to my oldest brother, and then later in the United Kingdom, where my other brother was born.

In Florida, my father and mother opened a business, Africana Gifts and Shells, a gift wholesaler and store that sold beautiful and unique seashells, handmade and carved wooden crafts, chimes, trinkets, and novelty items. Partners in everything — marriage, business, and parenting — my parents shared the division of labor. My father was a road warrior, traveling the world to comb beaches, collect shells, and buy stock for the store. Back in Florida, my mom ran the business and took care of her three sons. She was a full-time mom. She had no help. She *was* the help. She was Supermom.

My brothers and I were closer to our mom. She was always present, a constant. She was also easier-going, more fun to be around. My father was tougher, the disciplinarian, and he had a temper, a short fuse. I guess I would call him the boss. But both of them taught us that life was family and family was life.

At one point, I remember, the family hit hard times financially. Through our house's thin walls, I overheard heated conversations that grew into arguments laced with hushed words that I imagine were difficult if not humiliating for my father to express aloud, much less consider. Words such as *debt, creditors, bankruptcy.* And then, over time, my father somehow pulled us out of the financial abyss. Ultimately, my sense of him — my memory of that time — is of a man on the move, always leaving for or returning from a business trip, and always, *always* working. I rarely saw him at rest, don't recall him ever being relaxed.

"I have to work" is a phrase that resonates with me. I don't know if my dad ever spoke those exact words, but I associate that phrase with him. They inform my image of him. They define him. And, I admit, those words also define me.

I became a practicing Muslim in high school. We lived in a mostly white neighborhood, and I attended a Lutheran school for ten years, starting in elementary school. Even though my brothers and I were the only dark-skinned people around — no African American or Latino families lived nearby — I remember only a few racist taunts and hassles. But when I switched to a public high school for my junior and senior years, I experienced a different vibe in the hallways, the lunch room, at after-school events: an undercurrent, a kind of low-level xenophobia.

Around that time I began to pray. I knew, of course, that we were Muslims, but as a family, we weren't very religious. I never saw my dad pray. He called himself a "practical man," and as I remember, he would say that he didn't have time to pray at home or attend services at a mosque. He was too busy. My mom was more religious, and I do remember her praying on occasion.

As for me, I always had been fascinated by the idea of faith and began reading about different religions from an early age. I read extensively about Christianity in my free time, but I eventually found myself drifting toward Islam, my own faith. I remember fasting for the first time when I was twelve. Nobody asked me to do it; I just did it on my own. It felt right, it felt logical, and it felt true. It was what Muslims did.

I started praying, too. Once a day at first, and then twice, and then three times a day or more. I would read the Quran and the Bible, and I would compare and contrast verses. Those practices moved me, stirring my intellect and touching my heart in ways I'd never felt before. Slowly, in my own quiet way, I became more and more pious.

I didn't proselytize or flaunt my religion, but whether people knew me well or not, they identified me as Muslim. Christian friends, which meant basically everyone, expressed their honest concern.

"You're going to Hell, and I feel so bad," one friend said to me.

"Well, thanks. I guess."

"I feel terrible. I wish I could just convert you, because if I don't, well, I just feel so bad for your *soul.*"

"Really?"

"It sucks. I feel so bad."

*That can't be right,* I thought. *I can't be going to Hell just because I'm not Christian. How could an "all-merciful God" create six billion people and, just like that, predestine most of them to go to Hell? That's not right. That is not what God meant.*

At least not the God I believe in.

I remember the first day I entered Johnson Memorial Health Services, the place that would become my workplace, my refuge, my home away from home.

I step into a corridor of soft light and instantly feel the warmth. Hospitals can be dark, sullen, cold places, sterile and institutional. But as I walk down the hallway here, I feel strangely *embraced.* Like a refugee who has been taken in.

I tour this hospital with one of the office staffers, a young woman wearing slacks and a sweater. We walk slowly, as if taking a stroll through a park. The staffer exudes warmth herself. She gushes about her coworkers, whom she considers her extended family. She talks about patients, nurses, doctors, and the residents of Dawson itself. She has lived here her entire life, and she will never live anywhere else. She is so genuinely passionate about the town that she could double as the mayor or president of the chamber of commerce.

*This is exactly where I want to be,* I think.

I have wanted a small-town experience. I have longed for the familiarity and closeness of knowing your neighbors.

Dawson, Minnesota.

We have found it.

The young staffer leads me through the rest of the tour. We pass through the ER and the OR, then loop around and arrive at the hospital entrance. We stop in front of the check-in area.

"Wait," I say, looking around, getting my bearings. "You have the same check-in for the hospital and the clinic?"

"Yes," the staffer says. "That way if a patient from the clinic needs to be admitted to the hospital, she's already checked in."

My mouth must drop open because my tour guide grins.

"What?" she says.

"It's kind of brilliant," I say.

"Well, yeah. I mean, it feels sort of . . . obvious," she says. Then she blushes, and we both crack up.

We complete the tour, walking through the entire medical center — inpatient, outpatient, the nursing home housed in the building next door. Suddenly I realize: *This is a lot for one person to oversee.*

The one person being me.

*How am I going to do all this?*

That question bangs inside my head.

But then the enormity of my job description — clinic medical director and hospital chief of staff — begins to dissolve because I know this is exactly what I want. I will have my opportunity to practice dignified medicine.

The staffer and I go back inside the hospital entrance and into the waiting room. I digest her descriptions of the place and the answers to my questions, absorbing all I can. She introduces me to nurses, other support staff, and a doctor at the end of his shift who is on his way out, leaving to go to another small-town hospital because he works here only part-time.

"Everyone multitasks," my guide says. "That's common." She nods toward a nurse sitting behind a desk. "Jody out there also works half-time on her farm. One of our other staffers works on the EMT service. And so on."

"Everybody shares," I say.

"Yep," she says. "That's the way it is here in Dawson."

We double back now, go past the nurses' station, toward the emergency room. As we walk, new ideas flood into my mind, improvements that could be made to the medical center. I've been told that the hospital board is open to innovation, prides itself on being progressive. I read constantly and keep abreast of the latest advances in medical technology. I would want to bring cutting-edge equipment here. I would begin small and, for example, for starters, suggest spending less than twenty thousand dollars on a new BiPAP machine that will allow patients who are crashing to breathe without a ventilator, keeping them out of the ICU and possibly keeping them alive.

In addition to technology, I would put an emphasis on preventive medicine — in particular dealing with obesity, which I see as a health crisis. I would introduce a bariatric clinic that specializes in weight loss. We need to reform people's thinking, especially in rural America. We need to get this population to commit to losing weight, eating healthier, and exercising.

The staffer must pick up on my daydream, because she asks, "So how does it feel, being here?"

I snap out of my reverie, take in the earnest, welcoming faces.

"It feels good," I say. "It feels — right."

Then, bizarrely, as if I've walked into the middle of a TV hospital drama, someone calls a code. The nurse practitioner on call barges through the emergency room doors, out of breath, her face flushed.

"Sorry to bother you, Dr. Virji," she says. "We always have a doctor on backup, but we're caught between shifts. We have an emergency atrial fibrillation, as in, right now, and —"

"You need help?"

"Thank you," she says, and I follow her into the ER.

Later, when Musarrat asks me about the interview at the hospital, I can't keep myself from laughing.

"What happened?" she asks me.

"I actually helped the nurse practitioner resuscitate a patient."

"Seriously? How did that go?"

"The patient did well."

"Thank God," Musarrat says.

"Yeah. I guess you'd say this interview was . . . different."

Johnson Memorial makes me an offer, and I accept. A short time later, Musarrat and I schedule a return to Dawson to look for a house. At the last minute, Musarrat comes down with the flu and I go myself.

I immerse myself in Dawson. I eat breakfast daily at Wanda's Diner, spending time with Wanda herself, an endearing, flamboyant woman who puts in fourteen-hour days, baking, cooking, waiting tables, and scrubbing her kitchen spotless. After breakfast, I spend hours each day looking at houses with a real estate agent. I see nothing that I like or that could accommodate our family of five. I start to panic, realizing that we may have to build a house, so I meet with a contractor and architect. They seem as though they would do a good job, but the financial cost of building a house from scratch, not to mention the emotional aggravation that always accompanies any kind of construction or remodeling, worries me. I tell them I need some time to think about it.

The night before I leave, I go to the Rusty Duck, the only restaurant in Dawson that serves dinner. I sit at a table near the bar, picking at my plate of fried mozzarella sticks, a basketball game flickering on a large TV screen across from me, when John and Ginger, a couple I haven't met, come over and introduce themselves.

"Hey, are you the new doctor?" John says.

"I am," I say and introduce myself.

"We need a good doctor," Ginger says.

"And someone's who full-time," John says.

"Hopefully I'll be both," I say. "Well, I promise I'll be full-time."

They laugh, and Ginger asks, "What are

you doing here now?"

"Actually, I'm looking for a place to live. I'd like to buy a house, but I haven't found anything."

They look at each other, and John says, "We're going to be selling our place. Why don't you look at it?"

"Really? Wow. Which house is it?"

"The yellow house right behind the old law offices."

I know it immediately. Victorian. Stunning.

"I've seen that house," I say. "It looks great from the curb."

"Come by tomorrow," Ginger says. "Ten o'clock?"

"Thank you. I'll be there."

The next morning, I enter the yellow Victorian house on Pine Street greeted by the smell of freshly baked blueberry muffins. Ginger hands me a plate with a muffin and a mug of coffee, and she and John walk me through their house: four bedrooms, three baths, kitchen with a center island, formal dining room, cared for, comfortable, pristine.

Home.

I take dozens of pictures and email them to Musarrat, who gives me her blessing. The rest of the transaction happens whiplash fast, and before I can catch my breath, we are the proud owners of the yellow Victorian house on Pine Street in Dawson, Minnesota.

After we've settled in Dawson, I meet Stacey Lee, the new CEO of Johnson Memorial. Within a stunningly short period of time, we make the leap from colleagues to friends. We just click.

"The first time we met, I was stunned by how young you look," Stacey tells me. "I almost blurted out, 'How old are you? You look about twelve.' "

I connect to her sense of humor, her intelligence, and her commitment to upgrading and expanding the medical complex. We also relate to each other because of what some may call coincidence and others may call destiny or karma: Stacey grew up in the yellow Victorian house on Pine Street, the house we bought and now live in.

"Wait, what?" I say. "We're sharing the same *house.*"

"My room was your daughter, Maya's, room," she says.

Stacey and I also share the same sensibility and point of view about life and family and, even though we don't talk about it much initially, politics. In fact, to my surprise, nobody in Dawson talks about the upcoming presidential election. At least not around me. I follow all the candidates' debates, watch the coverage of the conventions, and stay informed about the issues, my emotions alternating between feeling sickened and enraged when the Republican presidential candidate Donald Trump spews hatred toward Muslims. But other than Stacey, nobody else I work with seems concerned or even remotely engaged. The election seems distant, as if it's happening somewhere else, in a different country, not our own.

"What is that about?" I ask Stacey one day.

"People don't want to bring anything bad out into the open," she says. "We keep our feelings private. We always put up a good front. It's called 'Minnesota nice.' "

"Minnesota *nice?*"

"Yeah. Hopefully everyone has good intentions, so let's hold hands and everything will be okay. We'll get through the bad spots if we work hard and smile and be *nice* to each other."

I blink at her, trying to read her. I think Stacey's being real, not at all sarcastic, and then she clarifies, "In other words, let's not bring any bad stuff out into the open."

But I know how Stacey really feels about

the election. As time goes on, we talk more and more about it. It becomes a running conversation, a subject of confusion and then anxiety —

*Donald Trump cannot be elected president. It can't happen. Can it?*

Stacey feels just as appalled and outraged by the candidacy of Donald Trump as I do and one day wears a pantsuit to work to show her support for Hillary Clinton. Behind closed doors, we rant about the presidential debates, Trump's offensive outbursts concerning a disabled reporter and a Gold Star family. We express our outrage and disbelief over the *Access Hollywood* tape. We're alone, though. Nobody else talks about the election. Conversations about politics — and religion — appear to be out of bounds. One day, I ask Stacey if she thinks any of the people who work with us at the hospital — our coworkers, the people I interact with, rely on, and have grown to like — would vote for Trump.

"Maybe," she says. "It's possible."

"It is?" I say. "Really?"

Stacey shrugs.

"Minnesota nice," she says.

Life seems to fast-forward. I picture our first days in Dawson, then the first weeks, the first months, and before I can catch my breath, we have come to the end of our first year.

The novelist Chaim Potok said all beginnings are difficult. Ours was. We went through the transition of remodeling our house, of living in a hotel for months. Then, finally, we moved into our house and settled in.

More than a year later, we survived our first brutal western Minnesota winter, slushed through the early spring thaw, sweated through a scorching summer, all of it made tolerable because of the acceptance, good cheer, and kindness of our neighbors.

Dawson has become our home. The kids and the cats have staked out their individual territories in our house. The kids have acclimated themselves to school and found friends. Musarrat has opened her salon and receives compliments on her work along with a steady flow of customers. Socially, we've found a comfort zone, making friends and entertaining often.

And I have found my place professionally. I am the doctor I have always wanted to be. I serve this rural community in the way I have always intended to, giving each patient the time he or she needs, committing to them for the long haul. Here in Dawson, for the first time in my career, I can offer my patients a "medical home."

I fall into a routine at work, or as close as I can get to one. I wear two or three hats — chief of staff at the hospital, head of its newly founded bariatric clinic, and founder and CEO of Body Togs, a weight loss product and diet program I started some time ago that has recently started to take off. To deal with the increasing demand for our products, I install my friend Doug as operations manager and rent a building across the street from the grocery store to serve as our corporate headquarters and warehouse. I intend to purchase the building in the future.

Every day, I try to set up my work schedule so I can make it home for dinner with the family. Typically, I begin work by eight and see about twelve patients in the clinic. I will usually see another two or three in the hospital and then visit one or two in the nursing home. Of course, when I'm on call every other week or so, for twenty-four or thirty-six straight hours, anything can happen — from hours of quiet and boredom to dealing with a trauma patient, inevitably at three in the morning. Despite the busyness, though, life in every sense is good.

I think about a patient I'll call Tom.

When I meet Tom at the bariatric clinic, he is carrying 260 pounds on his five-foot, nine-inch frame. Tom suffers from idiopathic pulmonary fibrosis, a chronic and irreversible lung disease for which there is no cure. In order to survive, he needs a lung transplant. Unfortunately, no surgeon will touch Tom because of his weight. He needs to lose 80 pounds to have the surgery.

Tom has tried numerous diets and checked into several clinics. Nothing has worked. He has not been able to maintain any meaningful weight loss. He's become frustrated, despondent, and scared. He doesn't know what to do. He fears he will die. Someone refers him to our bariatric clinic, and Tom comes to us as a last resort, his version of a Hail Mary pass.

I tell Tom about our program.

"It's different," I say. "I describe it as eighty percent knowledge and twenty percent effort. It takes a little bit of time to understand it, but once you've got it, and you will, you'll find it's probably easier than anything else you've tried. Now, it's not effort*less*. You will have to put in some work."

"I'm open. I'm eager. What do we do first?"

I explain that we'll start by doing a metabolic intake and an inventory of all of the medications Tom is taking. Many medications actually stimulate the appetite, so if he is taking any of those, we'll prescribe an alternative. Once we determine his medical conditions and get his meds under control, we'll put him on our diet, which is informed by the latest research in nutrition. The good news is that Tom doesn't have to weigh or measure his food or count calories. The program is more about learning to navigate the food choices all of us have to make in the average supermarket.

"We'll tell you which specific brands you can eat in all different foods," I tell Tom. "We break it down: breads, pasta sauce, frozen meals, and so on. What you eat matters as much as how much you eat."

"Okay," he says, nodding, taking it all in.

"We're also going to fit you with wearable leg weights. You strap them on in the morning, go about your day, take them off at night. It's like running two miles a day without realizing it."

"Wow," Tom says. And then he asks quietly, "I don't want to put you on the spot . . . but do you think you can help me?"

"Absolutely."

He swallows, nods, and says with difficulty, "How much weight do you think I might be able to, you know, lose?"

"I promise I will be accountable, Tom, but I can't promise an exact number."

"I understand." He hesitates, then blurts, "Give me a ballpark."

"Our patients lose, on average, about eight pounds a month."

"I'll take that in a heartbeat," Tom says.

After adjusting Tom's medications, we put him on our diet and set him for his next appointment a month later. That day, the nurse weighs him as I look on. Tom has lost ten pounds.

From that moment on, Tom becomes passionate about our program, our poster child. Nine months later, he strides over to the scale looking like a completely different person.

He steps up, and I see he weighs 180 pounds.

I smile. Then I tell him some incredible news.

"Tom, the surgeon wants to hold off on the surgery."

"What? Why? I thought I'd lost enough weight."

"You have. But your lung function has actually gotten better. The surgeon wants to wait to see if your lungs continue to improve."

"Is this — normal?"

"No," I say. "It's unusual." Then I add, "It's pretty great."

Tom lowers his head, nods, and starts to cry. I put my hand on his shoulder and bite my lip because I'm about to lose it, too.

And then we're both so overwhelmed that we hug.

It's been nearly four years since the bariatric clinic opened. I knew that Dawson and the surrounding areas needed a program like this, but the demand has gone way past my expectations. At last count, we were down a total of 3,500 pounds for our patients. New patients have to wait six weeks to see me. I see patients from towns thirty minutes to an hour away, and I have some people who come from the Twin Cities, three hours away. I have one patient who drives all the way from Kansas, an eight-hour round trip. She says she doesn't mind the drive, that it's a small price to pay to improve the quality of her life.

I consider working with my bariatric patients, people like Tom, part of living a life of goodness. Or as we Muslims call it, Sharia law.

"You're the face of the town," my friend Jason says one night after dinner.

"Oh, come on."

"No, seriously. People see you all the time, in town, at Wanda's, at school, at concerts, at the hospital. You're visible. You're public."

Jason grins and adds, his eyes narrowing, "You're famous."

"Oh, please. That's the last thing I am."

"It's not a bad thing to be the face of the town. You have a decent face."

"A brown face. A Muslim face."

Jason makes a fist in front of his mouth, miming a microphone, deepening his voice like a TV news anchor. "Dr. Ayaz Virji, slowly dragging Dawson into the twenty-first century. Taking baby steps."

"As long as we're taking some kind of steps. Forward steps."

I dig under the couch cushions, searching for the remote, find it lodged in a crack, wriggle it out, aim at the cable box, and fire up Netflix.

*"Daredevil,"* Jason says, as the theme music comes up.

Jason teaches social studies at our middle school. Wiry and smart, he is one of the few people I've met whose energy level rivals my own. When we first met three years ago, we discovered a mutual obsession with *Star Wars* and superheroes, embraced each other as the good and true nerds we are, and started hanging out, mostly at our house, Jason usually arriving with one or more of his four kids. I'm not sure when we first started talking politics — probably as we switched out DVDs during a *Star Wars* marathon — but we quickly discovered, to our mutual relief, that we shared the same opinion of Donald Trump, the candidate — fear, dread, loathing, and the absolute certainty that our country could never possibly elect him president. As the weeks go by, we're becoming less sure of that last part.

"I have to ask you something," Jason says one night. "You went to Georgetown and Duke and ended up *here*?"

I laugh. "Yeah."

"What happened? Did you do something bad?"

"Witness protection, man."

"Oh, okay, I'll back off."

"I wish I could talk about it."

We both crack up, and as we settle in and begin to fall under the spell of *Daredevil,* I remember Jason describing the first time he saw me.

"I hadn't met you yet," he said. "It was at the school, and I saw you, Musarrat, and Maya coming out of the building. The two of you were standing on either side of your daughter, and you were each holding one of her hands. I immediately experienced this incredible connection, and I thought, 'These people look different than everyone else in town, and I see so much love. This little thing. This moment. Why can't the media show this?' "

Then Jason thought, "I want you here. We need you here. And not just as a doctor."

# 4
## JIHAD

---

*Jihad.*

The media — and those who just don't know — believe this to be an ugly word.

Fox News has defined *jihad* as a holy war.

But that is false.

Literally, *jihad* means "struggle."

I am not in a war, holy or otherwise.

But it is fair and accurate to say that sometime in the very first hours of Wednesday, November 9, 2016, when I learned that Donald Trump had been elected president of the United States and that 65 percent — nearly two-thirds — of the people in our county had voted for him, living in Dawson became my struggle.

My jihad.

The evening begins with a growing sense of excitement as Musarrat and I tune in to the election returns in our living room. I'm not superstitious, but I don't dare express aloud what I'm feeling. We are about to witness history. We are about to witness the election of the first woman president.

Slowly — unbearably slowly — the results start coming in, state by state. We switch from network to network, mostly from CNN to MSNBC, occasionally tuning in to a Minneapolis station to track our local results. As we hear the disbelief trickling into Rachel Maddow's and Brian Williams's voices and switch back and forth to a CNN anchor standing baffled in front of his color-coded digital maps, I feel a sinkhole forming in my stomach.

"I can't believe this," I say as the clock flips to midnight and we cross into Wednesday, November 9. At around one-thirty in the morning, stunned, devastated, upset, we trudge upstairs and retreat to our bedroom.

We prepare for sleep, but I'm too agitated to get into bed. Instead, feeling like a wounded, caged animal, I pace. Musarrat, propped by pillows against our headboard, eyes me, following me, a pained and helpless look on her face.

"I'm just —" I really don't know how to complete that sentence. I feel so many emotions: anger, fear, dread, disbelief, impotence, and betrayal. I think I feel that most of all. A deep sense of betrayal.

"We live with these people," I say, practically moaning in pain. "How could they vote for him? They're voting against *us*. They're repudiating *us*."

"Ayaz . . . ," Musarrat says quietly.

My anger builds. I slash toward the window with my hand.

"This is really happening," I say, my breath huffing. "I don't believe it. Oh, my God. This *idiot*."

"You need to calm down," Musarrat says.

I keep pacing. I keep huffing. I raise my voice. I can feel the heat flaming in my cheeks.

"Don't these people see? Are they all blind? What is the matter with them?"

"Ayaz, please, keep your voice down, the neighbors."

By two in the morning, all the news outlets make it official: Donald Trump has won the presidency; Hillary Clinton has lost.

My rage has reached new levels. I can't contain myself.

"We can't stay here," I say to Musarrat. "We have to leave."

"Your parents are coming in the morning." Musarrat squints at the bedside clock. "In a few hours."

"I know, I know."

I pace. I walk faster. Then, my voice erupting in pain, I ask, simply, "Why?"

In life, I always try to stay two steps ahead, aiming to keep a solid backup plan in place in case, God forbid, something terrible happens. I don't want to be hyperbolic — I want to be realistic, pragmatic — but it feels that with the election of Donald Trump, the doomsday scenario has happened. Or at least that the machinery has turned on and begun churning.

The morning after the election, I call my brother in Dubai.

"What happened?" we ask each other simultaneously.

"I don't know," I say. "I feel so ambushed, so betrayed. These people are my patients. My neighbors. My friends. Two-thirds of them voted for Trump. Who *are* these people?"

"You have to move here," my brother says. "Just send out your résumé and you'll have dozens of offers, guaranteed, done deal."

"I know," I say. "I already get job offers. I keep turning them down."

"And I'll get you a place to live. You'll have many options. Give me a day. Less."

My brother, who works in real estate, has often said that all I have to do is give him the word and he will set us up with a beautiful place to live in Dubai. At the moment, this seems like a no-brainer. I want to get out of Dawson. I want to flee.

I've managed a total of maybe three hours of sleep. After my morning prayers, I make two phone calls. First, I call Musarrat's cousin Rahil, a medical student, whom I have recruited to join me in Dawson. Rural America remains in desperate need of doctors, and Johnson Memorial has offered Rahil a position after he's completed his residency.

"Rahil," I say on the phone, "it's not safe for you to come here."

"You think it's that bad?"

"Donald Trump is our president. I'm going to leave."

"But I've signed all the paperwork —"

"Go to Canada. Go to Dubai. Rahil, they want to put Muslims on a registry. I'm telling you, I'm leaving. I will not stay here. I'm *not* staying here."

I guzzle a cup of coffee, and then, still fuming, I follow Musarrat into the living room as she moves to the desk where we keep mail, a computer, keys. I continue the rant I've been on for the last seven hours. "How can we stay here? The people voted two to one for Trump. That's two to one against us. Those people are my patients.

Don't they get it?"

Musarrat picks up the car keys, jiggles them absently for a moment, and says, "We'll do what we have to do, you know that. We'll discuss what's right for the family. I just don't want to react in haste, okay?"

I sigh. "You're right."

"Now I'm going to the Cities to pick up your parents."

I shake my head. "What timing, huh? Great introduction to Dawson. I wish I were in a better mood."

"You could take a personal day, stay home, or go in later —"

"The doctor takes a sick day? I don't think so."

Musarrat comes over and throws her arms around me. We hold on to each other for a long time, clinging to each other. Finally, gently, we break apart.

"We'll figure it out, you know that, right?" she says.

"I know."

"And I know this is different."

We kiss, and Musarrat, my wife, my partner, tightens her head scarf and heads out of our house in Dawson to pick up my parents at the airport outside Minneapolis, three hours away.

■ ■ ■ ■

I pace, and the more I pace, the worse I feel. I think about my journey here, my choice to come to this tiny town to serve an underserved rural population. In three short years, we have changed so much in this community. I've given my patients so much personal attention. We've upgraded equipment in the hospital. The bariatric center has a waiting list. I feel as if I have truly changed lives.

*But they don't care about me,* I think. *They see me only as a doctor. They don't see me as a person. What will this community do if I leave?*

I pace . . . and inside my head, my thoughts swirl. The anger intensifies, seeps into my mind. I rant to myself.

*I'm done. You want this guy as your president? You want to put people who look like me and my family on a registry? You think we're terrorists? Fine. I'll leave. Good luck to you. I'm out.*

I call the real estate agent who sold us our house and leave a message on her voice mail. "Rose, this is Dr. Virji. I want to put our house on the market, effective immediately. We need to sell as soon as possible. We're leaving. Again, I want to sell *immediately.* Please call me back so we can do all the necessary paperwork ASAP. Thank you" — and I can't resist adding, "Have a nice day."

Even though it feels as though I've already walked five miles just by pacing inside my house, I decide to walk to work. Maybe it'll help me blow off steam. I start walking from our front door on Pine Street, heading toward the hospital's back entrance fifteen minutes away. The brisk morning breeze bites my cheeks. I duck inside my coat collar and quicken my pace to a near run, but as I approach the hospital, I don't feel calmer, I feel more agitated, more upset. I feel worse.

I barge into the hospital as if I have been launched. I stride down the hallway, my rage palpable, pulsing in the pit of my stomach.

The first person I see is a member of our office staff. For the most part, everyone at the hospital avoided talking politics during the campaign, but I know she voted for Hillary Clinton. Her eyes misty, she shakes her head.

"I can't believe what happened," she says.

"I honestly don't know what I'm going to do," I say, my back stiffening.

"What . . . what do you mean?"

"I have to seriously rethink things."

"But, Dr. Virji —"

"I am so angry," I say, realizing that those words don't come close to describing the rage I feel.

I come to Mitch, a staffer, a decent, hardworking guy who voiced his support for Trump. He must not read the dark look on my face because he tilts his head and says, "Hey, Dr. Virji, happy Wednesday."

"What's so happy about it, Mitch?"

I can't help myself. I want to argue with him. I want to pick a fight.

"Aw, come on. It's going to be all right," he says.

"It's going to be all *right*?"

A few other people drift toward us. I begin to speak, quietly at first, and then slowly my voice rises into some kind of crazed crescendo. "You guys — the people here in Dawson, my home, where *I live* — voted for a guy who wants to put me on a Muslim registry. *Sixty-five percent* of the *county* voted for Trump. You voted for a guy who promotes hate. You voted for a sexual predator who I wouldn't allow within a hundred yards of my house."

"My bad," Mitch says. "You should never talk about religion or politics at work."

88

"This isn't about politics, Mitch. It's about morality — and decency."

I storm off.

I feel Mitch and the others staring at my back.

I have a reputation for almost always being in a good mood, for joking around. I don't generally lose it. Of course, I've had moments when I've gotten upset and, yes, even angry, but that's usually when I've been on call for twenty-four hours straight. Nobody has seen me like this before.

I go into my office and hang up my coat. A few seconds later, my office manager and Jordan, my nurse, appear at the door. I see the concern on their faces. The office manager, her voice low and shaky, says, "A lot of us are sad."

"It's going to be okay," Jordan says, echoing Mitch, setting me off.

I raise my head slowly and stare. I have never raised my voice at Jordan before, but I can feel that something inside me has snapped.

"You want to know what I really think?"

She doesn't want to know. She just wants to back out of my office. She takes a tentative step in that direction, but my look freezes her.

"Let me state this again." I hold, and then

I hiss, "You don't care about us. The only reason you care about me is that I have an MD after my name. That's why I've been welcomed into this community. If you could take the *brownness* or the *Muslim-ness* out of me and put that part of me on a registry and somehow keep the doctor part of me, you would."

Jordan's bottom lip trembles, and then she bursts into tears. She turns and runs out, the office manager following. I exhale, trying to calm my pounding heart. I sink into my desk chair and lower my head into my hands.

After a few minutes, I gather myself and open my laptop. I email my brother, telling him to look for places for us to live in Dubai; then I dash off a cover letter and send out my résumé. I take a deep breath and then compose an email to Stacey Lee. I tell her that, effective immediately, I resign my position at Johnson Memorial. I stare at the email for a moment, my mouth feeling dry, my fingers poised above the keyboard. But then my anger pulses hot, and I hit "send."

I have several patients to see in the clinic, including my first appointment with Pastor

Mandy, the new interim pastor at Grace Lutheran Church. For the briefest moment, I consider rescheduling the rest of the day and going home, but what would I do there? Sulk? Stare at the walls? Pace some more?

I glance at the clock on my home screen and see that I still have a few minutes before I meet Pastor Mandy. I charge out of my office, roar down the hall to Stacey's office. I find her seated at her desk. I shut the door and begin to pace.

"I read your email," Stacey says.

I nod, pulling up in front of her desk.

"Yes," I say, and then I reiterate, "I'm resigning my chief of staff and medical directorship positions."

"I know you're furious. But I don't accept your resignation."

I sigh heavily, stare at my hands. "This feels so unreal."

"I considered wearing black today," Stacey says.

"That would've made a statement," I say.

"The *United* States of America," she says. "We're anything but."

"I only saw a few Trump signs in Dawson. And then you wake up and —"

My voice trails off.

"Yep. I know. A lot of quiet support. *Minnesota nice.*"

Stacey taps her hands on her desk. She gazes past me, cranes her neck, and looks out the window.

"Everyone is so self-absorbed," she says. "I know you think this is all about you, but it's not. People only care about themselves, about their own issues."

"I know. And that's why I have to leave."

Neither of us speaks, the silence feeling like a wound.

"Where will you go?" Stacey says.

I shrug and say, "Dubai," and then I resume pacing in front of Stacey's desk. My body feels electrified. "Stacey, I've told you. After 9/11, I experienced Islamophobia firsthand. I am not putting my wife and kids through that again."

"I can't imagine what that was like," Stacey says. "I know how horrifying this must be. I'm terribly upset, but I know it can't be as deep for me. It just can't. They didn't say all white females between the ages of forty and fifty are going to be put on a registry and deported."

"That's right," I say. I check my watch and whirl toward the door. "I have a patient."

"Ayaz, I don't want you to go, but I'll support any decision you make."

"I don't see how I can stay."

■ ■ ■ ■

The morning after the election, Mandy France wants to stay in bed. She stares at the ceiling, feeling numb, lifeless, and unfathomably depressed. After a few moments, Kelly, her husband, rustles beside her, groans, rolls over, and squints at her.

"Is Trump still president?" he asks.

"Let me check."

Mandy grabs her phone from the nightstand and glances at a recent news alert lit up in green.

"Yep," she says.

"I'm going back to sleep," Kelly says.

"I wish we could sleep for the next four years," Mandy says.

Eventually Mandy struggles to a sitting position, scrolls through today's schedule on her phone, confirms that she has an appointment at the clinic, and drags herself out of bed. She knows that today has all the makings of a very hard day. She decides that because she feels so vulnerable and genuinely sad she will screen her calls and try not to talk to anyone who might unduly — or even unknowingly — upset her. A second after she makes that decision, her phone rings. She sees it's Pastor Kendall's wife calling from Grace Lutheran Church. She answers after the first ring.

"What are we going to do?"

"Pray," Pastor Mandy says. "Might as well start there."

On her way to the clinic, Mandy stops at the church office to commiserate about the election with someone other than her husband.

"My first thought, honestly?" Pastor Kendall's wife says to Mandy, now in person. "I wonder how the Virjis are taking this."

"I know," Mandy says. "I'm actually on my way to an appointment with Dr. Virji right now."

"I'm not sure you can ask him."

"I know. What would I say?"

I try to calm myself before going into the examination room. I take a couple of cleansing breaths, murmur some words of prayer. Then I put my shoulder into the door and enter the room. I introduce myself to Pastor Mandy, the intern at Grace Lutheran Church. We shake hands and I put on the best, most professional face I can. Smiling, warm, welcoming — fake.

*I'm not fooling her,* I think. *She can see right through me. She can probably see the smoke coming out of my ears.*

Somehow I settle myself. I sit on the rolling stool next to the exam table, flip through her chart, and glance at her medical history. This is a preliminary meeting. I will be asking questions, doing an intake, giving information, discussing a plan, a direction.

We begin to talk. I jot a few notes, check off the appropriate boxes. I keep my hand steady as I write, but I can't keep my leg from shaking.

*Musarrat was right,* I think. *I should've stayed home today.*

I talk about how the clinic works. I go through the basics of our program. I explain our philosophy, the highlights of our diet, the suggested supplements, the medically documented approach and overall health benefits, the commitment patients are expected to make, and the time frame we can anticipate to achieve the kind of results we want. I indicate how our program differs from other programs. I talk about my experience, explain my credentials, my training. I know I've gone quickly, perhaps even rushed. Given the events of today, distracted by my parents arriving, the election, my emotions careening from low-level anger to pulsating rage to high anxiety, thinking about the future, the country's future, my *kids'* future — I hope I've been halfway comprehensible. I blow out a thin column of air and ask Mandy if she has any questions.

"Oh, no, I get it. So, okay, you're certified —"

"Um-hm," I say, feeling a twinge of impatience. "Board certified."

"And also certified in family practice as well?"

I pause and look at her. "I'm not sure what you're trying to say, but, yes, I'm a real doctor."

I don't remember much else of that first meeting. Everything has been lost in a cloud of emotion. In a blur, I say good-bye to Mandy, agreeing to set our next appointment, extend my hand in a quick, tentative handshake, trying to squash the wave of anger — at this day, this election, this *president* — that suddenly overwhelms me and propels me out of the room.

*He seems like a nice guy,* Mandy thinks. *Maybe a little intense. He's kind of like a human whirlwind.*

I can barely work. I see a few more patients, tamping down my anger while I'm with them but feeling myself about to explode the second I leave them. I decide it's best to avoid people as much as possible, and I try to lose myself in paperwork. That doesn't work, either. I stare blankly at my computer screen, the images on my desktop dancing and melding into a blotch of cloudy and painful colors. I leave my office and head into the corridor, where I see one of the staff members crying.

"Dr. Virji," she says, her voice halting. "Please don't go."

Wow. Word spreads fast. I charge into Stacey's office and find her at her desk.

"I'm sorry to barge in on you," I say.

She waves the thought away. "It's all right. Anytime. You know that. Especially today." She heaves a huge sigh. "I know you don't drink, but I sure could use something."

"People are crying out there."

I must appear confused because Stacey peers up at me. "It's because of you. They're in shock. They think you're leaving."

"Well, I am. I've called a Realtor —"

"Ayaz, please. Take some time. A few days. Talk to Musarrat. Weigh all your options. Really think about this. Having said all that, I'll support any decision you make."

"Okay," I say. "I will."

Stacey looks at me, and her eyes start to fill up. "Ayaz, so, *so* many people care about you and your family. You may not believe it right now, but this is your home."

■ ■ ■ ■

I seek out my nurse, Jordan, and apologize for my outburst. I try to explain that for me today has turned out to be a sick day — in addition to feeling deeply, uncontrollably angry and weirdly out of balance, I feel physically ill. I really should take Stacey's advice and go home. I would send any member of my staff home if he or she felt the way I do.

I do leave a couple hours early. Musarrat and my parents are on their way back from the airport, enjoying the three-hour ride from the Twin Cities, my parents mesmerized by the vast blue sky that seems to rest gently on the endless rolling green farmland of western Minnesota. This is their first visit to Dawson, and even though my mother will be having a medical procedure, I had hoped it would be a good trip. For the last two years, I have gushed about this place — the wonderful people, the quaintness of the town, the school — and bragged about the medical center. And now I'm planning to give it all up.

As I walk into town, my anger revs and I pick up my pace. I have brought so much to this community. I have brought in a business that has provided, at last count, seven new jobs, not insignificant in a town with a total population of fifteen hundred. And if I leave — *when* I leave — how will they replace me at the hospital? Qualified white doctors are not flowing into rural America. They're just not coming. All the doctors I have recruited to join me are people of color, born in India, Asia, the Middle East, Africa. The great irony is that as our new president proposes a travel ban with the intention of keeping immigrants out of our country, immigrants with medical degrees are the only ones coming to care for Americans out *in* the country.

*So ridiculous,* I think. *It's sick. And it's sad.*

I decide to walk through town, passing all the businesses I frequent — the barbershop, Wanda's Diner, the bowling alley, the smell of soybeans being processed at the nearby plant, a surprisingly pleasant smell that reminds me of freshly popped popcorn — and I wonder, how many of these people voted for Trump? Did Jim, who runs the bowling alley? Did the mayor, who cuts my hair and drives my kids in his school bus? Did Wanda?

As I turn down Pine Street, heading for my house, I catch a glimpse of Doug, who manages the grocery store across the street and works for me at Body Togs, jogging in my direction. Doug has become a trusted friend. When we started getting close with people here, we informed them that we have a drop-in policy at our house — an offer that Doug takes seriously, usually, I notice, around dinnertime. But this day, I have only the election on my mind. I stop suddenly and face Doug.

"Did you vote?" I say.

I know how I sound.

Accusatory. Impatient. Angry. But I can't help myself.

"I did," Doug answers, drawing himself up, towering over me.

"Well? Did you vote for Trump?"

*I'm not going to lie to him,* Doug thinks. *I haven't lied to him about anything. I tell him probably more than I tell anyone, more than I've ever told anyone. I don't lie to Ayaz. He is my friend.*

"Yes," Doug says. "I voted for him."

I spin around and settle in front of him, a scowl scorching my face.

"Why, Doug?" I say. "What the heck were you thinking, man?"

"I didn't see much of a choice," Doug says.

"Hillary is a lot better."

"Not to me."

"Why not to you?"

"I don't like her."

"Why?"

"She's a crook."

"*She's* a crook?"

"She has a dysfunctional family. We already had Bill —"

I feel my heart racing, my breath coming fast. I stammer. "Do you . . . *know* . . . how *offensive* it is that you voted for Trump? Do you know that you have personally offended me?"

Doug goes silent. The night comes on abruptly, suddenly, as it does here in Dawson, but before Doug's face becomes obscured in shadow, I see a deep hurt creasing his face.

"I didn't — I wasn't . . ." He pauses. "I didn't mean to offend you. That wasn't my intention at *all* —"

"It totally offends me," I say quickly, quietly.

Doug sniffs. "The only reason I voted for him was because I thought someone with that much money and that much arrogance and power . . . if he tells me that he's going to fix health care —"

Doug swallows and exhales, curls his lip. "Last year I had seventeen thousand dollars of medical expenses. That's seventeen thousand dollars out of my pocket. That's why I voted for him. That's the only reason."

"Where do you get that he knows anything about health care? He has not spent one minute in public service."

"He's run businesses. He's tough —"

"His businesses have all *failed,* Doug. Six bankruptcies. And he's not tough. He's a bully."

"I wanted to give him a chance," Doug says weakly.

"I'm going to leave," I say.

"What?"

"I'm not going to stay in Dawson. I'm going to move."

Doug looks stricken. "Where? Where would you go?"

"I don't know. Dubai, maybe."

"But the hospital, your kids, your friends —"

I look at him pointedly. "Some of my friends voted for Trump."

Doug nods, wipes his nose with the sleeve of his jacket. "Fine. I deserve that. But let me tell you something. Body Togs. Your company. *Our* company now?"

I laugh cynically. "You know I almost didn't bring that company in? I almost shut it down. I was this close to closing it down. Then I brought you in and now we've provided *seven jobs.* That is something in this town."

"It's a lot," Doug says, and then he says, softly, his voice halting, "You know how they ask this question all the time in politics, 'Are you better off now than you were a year ago?' "

"Yeah."

"Well, I am, because I work for you. And —" He swallows, and then he says, "Not just because of that. Because I got to know you. Because you're in my life."

For a long time, we say nothing. We stand fifty feet from my front door, two guys, immobilized, standing in silence, finally kicking at imaginary pebbles on the sidewalk, until Doug says, "At least I voted."

"Yeah. You exercised your right as a US citizen. I'll give you that."

"Okay," Doug says, rolling back on his heels, glancing over his shoulder toward his store. He looks unsure, unsteady, lost.

"Okay," I echo with a sigh. I turn and start walking toward my house. I stop when I realize that Doug hasn't moved. I look back. He's stayed behind, still standing on the sidewalk, slumped and weaving slightly from uncertainty. I gesture at my front door.

"Well?" I say.

He hesitates and shrugs, looking confused.

"Aren't you going to drop in?"

"Why is Daddy so angry?" Maya asks
Musarrat that night after dinner.

Doug has left, my parents have returned
to their bed-and-breakfast, and I'm back in
the living room, yelling at the TV.

"He's upset about the election," Musarrat
says, cuddling Maya, stroking her hair.
"Donald Trump isn't a good choice for us."

After a long pause, Faisal asks, half seriously, "Can't we just pretend we're not
Muslim?"

Later on, I leave another voice mail for
the real estate agent and send out a second
round of résumés, including for one of the
primary physicians at the US military base
in Qatar. Musarrat doesn't argue. She also
doesn't discourage me from expressing
myself loudly and emotionally, although at
one point she urges me not to shout toward
the window because the neighbors can hear
me.

At around eight o'clock, Jason stops over
unannounced with his twelve-year-old
daughter, Paige, and Austin, an aide at the
kids' school who has grown close with
Faisal.

"We thought you might want company,"
Jason says.

I give Musarrat a hard look.

"I didn't call them," she says. "They came on their own."

"You have an open-door policy," Jason says. "Your door was open, so —"

Austin laughs and crashes down on the couch next to Faisal, who's playing a video game. Faisal fusses around a stack of magazines on the coffee table, locates a second controller, and hands it to Austin.

"This election," Austin says, fumbling with the controller. "I'm so upset."

"We're going to move," I say stiffly. "We're probably going to Dubai."

A silence.

"Are you serious?" Jason says.

"A hundred percent," I say.

"I don't want to move," Faisal says in a small, pained voice, shaking his head. Faisal, fifteen, who has Asperger's syndrome, struggles with change, even the idea of it. He becomes especially nervous when he thinks about traveling.

I catch Musarrat's eye. She's giving me a hard look.

"What?" I say. "It's true."

Faisal slams back into the couch. "I'll only go if Austin comes with us," he says. We've often spoken of taking Austin with us on one of our visits to Dubai. In fact, Austin came up with the idea.

"I'd love to see Dubai," Austin said one day. "I have to come with you. I can help out."

"We're going to find you a nice Muslim girl," Musarrat said, laughing, teasing him.

"Perfect," Austin, a steadfast atheist, said. "I'll convert."

"Oh, my God, Austin," Musarrat said. "If you convert, that will be the end of us."

"People will think we made you do it," I said. "We would never be able to live here."

And now, the day after the election, looking at Faisal, sullen, upset, panicked that we may soon disrupt his routine and once again uproot him, I believe that we have no choice.

After Austin leaves and Faisal has gone upstairs to his room, and Musarrat, Maya, and Paige have retired to the dining room, Jason slides the original *Star Wars* movie, *Star Wars: A New Hope,* into our DVD player. We consider watching *The Empire Strikes Back,* the episode in which the imperial forces, the evil empire, win. Even though that mirrors our mood, I nix the idea.

"Yeah, we don't need to put more fuel on the fire," Jason says. "We need hope."

He plops down in front of the TV, his

hands circled around a mug of tea. I pace.

"Unreal, unreal, *unreal,*" I say. "I wish you knew how upset I am."

"I'm slow, but I'm getting a pretty good idea."

"It's so UNBELIEVABLE. He is so DISGUSTING."

*He's a human volcano,* Jason thinks, tracking me with his eyes.

"You're scaring me a little bit," he murmurs.

I stop pacing and crash down on the couch next to him.

"It's real, isn't it? It's really happening."

"I shouldn't even tell you this, but today in the cafeteria, some kids were chanting, 'Build the wall, build the wall!' "

"That's sick," I say.

"Not a lot. A few, though."

"You see why I have to leave, right?"

"This is so wrong," Jason says. "An ignorant person should not cause a smart person to leave their home. That should not happen."

"It's happening. People should be careful what they wish for." I pause in midpace. "I want to move *yesterday.* Mentally, I am out of here."

The movie begins, the iconic opening music distracting us for a few moments, and

107

then I catch Jason deep in thought. Finally he says, "I have a lot of stuff you gave me, well, things I borrowed from you. I have a whole bunch of spices of yours, from when I was making chili."

"Keep those. Keep them all. You can keep every spice in this whole house. We'll never get them through security."

"Your washing machine is much better than mine. I'll miss bringing my laundry over."

I shake my head, laugh. I will miss Jason, his irreverent sense of humor, his energy, his like-mindedness, his kindness.

"This may sound — whatever — but after the election, I needed somebody to talk to," Jason says. "You're it."

"I'm honored," I say. Then quietly, "Seriously, I know."

"The truth is, and I'm not going to look at you when I say this because it's corny and we're guys —" Jason pauses, says nothing for a while, but then turns and faces me directly and he says, "I really don't want my buddy to leave."

Two hours later, with the movie finished, Paige and Maya asleep, Jason picks up his daughter and starts to carry her to our front door, ready to sling her over his shoulder to take her to his car.

"Thanks," I say. "I needed that. You don't know how much."

"Me, too," Jason says and hesitates. "So, okay then. Tomorrow?"

"Yeah."

"Great," Jason says. "I'll see you tomorrow."

It takes five full days for Rose, the real estate agent, to return my call. She leaves me a voice mail, saying, "I just got your message. Unfortunately, I'm retired. I'm not doing this anymore. Sorry I can't help you sell your house. Good luck."

*She waited five days to return my call?* I think. *That seems almost premeditated, as if she was waiting for me to cool off. Smart.*

Because by now, six days after the election, the whole town knows I have decided to leave. In Dawson, the same as with the patrons of the bar in the TV sitcom *Cheers,* everybody knows your name . . . and your business . . . and no doubt your secrets. People talk. It's what people here do.

I not only know that, I embrace that. In fact, I want people to see a FOR SALE sign planted on our lawn in front of our house. I want everybody to see the change they voted for. I want them to see what they did. I want them to see how angry I am.

I have vented, raged, shouted, probably disturbed and upset my neighbors, and certainly upset my friends, my coworkers, my children, my parents, my wife, and myself. I sent out my résumé, looked for housing in Dubai, even went so far as to enroll our kids in school there. Musarrat, knowing me, supporting me, stood by me as I expressed my emotions, passionately, aloud, and *loud*. We discussed all our options, calmly and sometimes not so calmly, and she strongly voiced her own opinion and expressed her own conflicted emotions. The election upset her as much as it did me. She felt just as ambushed by the people in Dawson who voted for Donald Trump as I did, and she felt as hurt. She has planted roots here, for herself, and for our children, especially Faisal, at least for now.

I don't call another Realtor. I simmer, I stew, and then gradually, two weeks or so after the election, my pacing ceases, my fury subsides. I cool off. I no longer wear my anger like a coat. I become calmer. I become more — myself. Austin, Doug, and Jason continue to come around, but not every night. They see that the storm has passed, for now.

I know why I should leave Dawson, but I begin to make a mental checklist of reasons why I should stay, which I revise and revisit, usually very late at night or very early in the morning, while lying awake in bed.

I should stay because I made a commitment to Stacey and to my patients. I want to follow through on what I have started. I already see the profound impact the bariatric clinic has had on so many people, and I want to keep that going. I feel responsible for it. In many ways, I feel that we have just begun to address the epidemic of obesity in rural America. Patients who have had no success losing weight in other programs, even at highly regarded places such as the Mayo Clinic, are finding success under our care.

I should stay because the hospital has broken ground on a multimillion-dollar expansion, with seven million dollars alone dedicated to a new surgery center. I spearheaded this, with Stacey, and I can't abandon that. The surgery center has my stamp, my signature, incorporates my vision. Outreach surgeons have made a commitment to the surgery center because of me. I promised I would be here, that we would work together. They would be coming to Dawson for me.

I should stay because I love my staff, my nurses, the other doctors, and especially my patients.

And I need to stay for Faisal. My son has made friends and has discovered his passion: music and theater. The music and theater departments at Dawson's high school offer programs and productions several times during the year, and Faisal has become an active participant in them. He dreams of becoming a professional performer, of pursuing his interest in theater at college. For the first time, he has found his place: Dawson.

And I want to stay because of my friends. I don't know what I would do without them, especially Jason, Austin, and Doug. They have made me welcome, brought me into their lives, and stood by my side through every one of my meltdowns. They have never wavered, never doubted, and always accepted me. They may not practice their religions with the same intensity I practice mine, but they are holy men. They are gifts to me.

"You know, not everybody in Dawson is perfect," Jason says. "We have a few jerks, a smattering of both closeted and uncloseted racists, but most people here support you and actually *like* you."

"I know," I say.

"Well," Jason says, "they like Musarrat and

the kids."

I feel vulnerable. My future and my family's futures — our very lives — will be controlled by a president and his advisers, who have stated openly that they hate Muslims. *We are a cancer,* they've said. They have spoken those exact words.

One night, after I've begun compiling my mental checklist, I turn to Musarrat, my lip trembling, and I say, "I really don't know what to do, but I'm serious, I don't know how we can stay here."

My wife lowers her head, pauses, and when she raises her eyes to meet mine, I see that they are brimming with tears.

"Ayaz," she says, "I don't want to go. It would be so hard to move again."

"I know," I say, reaching for her hand. "It will be hard to leave."

"Ayaz," she says again through her tears, squeezing my hand, "I don't know if I can."

So for all those reasons, but especially for Musarrat and Faisal, we stay. A part of me also decides to stay as an act of defiance. Even as my anger eventually subsides from a full boil to a low, persistent simmer, I still feel disappointed in those who voted for Trump. I remain vigilant. I've lowered my expectations. I vow to be less naive. I have

113

to be. But I will not be driven from my home. I will not flee my own country.

# 5
## FALLOUT

A winter's day in Dawson.

Saturday morning around nine o'clock.

I step onto our front porch, carefully negotiate the icy steps and crunch along the sidewalk packed with snow, and go out to the street.

*When I get back from the store, I'll shovel that walk,* I think. *It's hazardous.*

The frigid morning air bites my ears and I pull my knit cap down. I cross the street and walk by the Carnegie Library building, headed to the grocery store to buy milk, bread, and bananas. These frequent walks from my house to the grocery store, a total of five minutes if I dawdle, remain one of the many pleasures I have living in Dawson. I can walk five minutes to basically any-where in town for milk, for a prescription, for a haircut, for breakfast, for fried moz-zarella sticks and a game of pool or to bowl a frame or two, or to pick up a book or read

115

a newspaper. Along the way, I can always count on friendly conversation with friends, with shop owners, with neighbors. We live in and share the same snug bubble. I admit that sometimes I like being inside our tiny bubble.

Today, even though it's just past nine o'clock, the sun seems high and bright, beating down in slants through the frigid morning air. I lower my head and absently clap my hands, my gloves making a sharp *smack* that actually startles me. And then, my head down as I walk, I see it. Directly in front of me. Facing me. Blocking my path.

A swastika.

On the sidewalk.

My mind immediately goes to Musarrat driving in her van, our two babies in the back seat, that bigot waving the baseball bat in the car behind her.

But that was seventeen years ago.

This is now.

This is here.

I stand over the swastika, staring at it, trying to blink it away, and I mutter, "This isn't happening."

That was months before Trump spoke to a crowd in Charlottesville, Virginia, after a neo-Nazi march resulted in a murder, gesturing, saying, "Some very fine people

116

on both sides . . ."

I kneel.

I reach my hand out to the swastika. I want to see if someone has drawn it with chalk or painted it.

I hesitate.

My fingers freeze an inch above it.

This symbol of brutality, of murder, of annihilation, of raw unbridled hatred.

I stare at it.

My hand lowers, and I touch it. It feels — gritty. As if it has been carved into the cement.

I touch it again.

Yes. Someone has taken a rock — or a hard object with a jagged edge — and etched the swastika into the sidewalk.

I reach into my pocket, pull out my phone, and take a picture. I send the picture to Musarrat, to Mandy, and to my friend Doug.

Then I stand and look over my left shoulder. I want to see how close I am to my house.

Fifty yards away, if that.

*What am I doing?*

*What will it take for me to leave?*

*Does something have to happen to my family?*

The questions barrel into me, pummel

me, and a fuse ignites within me. I feel my anger rise.

I don't want to squelch my anger. I want it to roar.

I want the anger to burn.

I practically sprint into the closest store. I find the owner — I'll call him Joseph — stocking shelves.

"Joseph, I need to show you something outside."

Joseph follows me outside. I turn the corner and stop next to the swastika.

"Wow," Joseph says.

"Yeah, well, this is what you get when you have a bigoted president," I say.

He says nothing for a count of five, and then, in a low wounded voice, he says, "Not everybody who voted for him is a bigot."

"You voted for him?"

"I did," Joseph says, rising to his full height and tucking his shirt into his pants. I see that his nose and cheeks have turned pink.

"It's cold," he says.

Rubbing his hands, he pivots and heads back inside the store. I follow close behind. He immediately turns to me. "Do you have a problem with me?" He opens his mouth, starts to say something else, changes his mind, reverses course, nods toward the street, and says, "Do you think I had something to do with *that* because I voted for Trump?"

"I don't have a problem with you," I say. "But I have a problem with this guy, with this president, and with these kinds of things that keep happening."

He sniffs. "I didn't vote for him because of those things."

"That's fine," I say. "But these things are real and they're happening. And he espouses hatred."

Joseph puts his hands on his hips. "Don't you think the community supports you?"

"Of course they do. The community supports the town doctor. They support this doctor who came from two thousand miles away to a town that nobody else wanted to come to. This community also voted to put this brown Muslim part of me on a registry."

"Don't you think this type of racism was here before?"

I want to scream. I want to swipe everything off his shelves with my arm. But I look at him, looking at me, and I see that he is actually trying to engage me and even perhaps to understand. He appears so earnest and so . . . helpless.

I suddenly feel sad and defeated. For some reason, I want to give him some sense of what I feel.

"Yes, Joseph," I say. "Racism has always been around and will always be around. But it's not a coincidence that after the election of Donald Trump, Islamophobic crimes increased, three mosques were burned down, and a hundred and fifty Jewish centers got bomb threats. All after the election."

"I told you, I didn't vote for him because of that. It was more that I voted against *her*."

"Look," I say, nodding in the direction of the street, "this is hurtful. And I didn't mean to insinuate that you did it. I know you didn't do it. The main thing is that it's *there*. It's real. It's right outside. Since the election, I have gotten death threats. Those are real, too. The nasty letters I get are real. The person who chased my wife years ago with a baseball bat was real. When something like this happens in my town? It shakes me."

"I can understand —"

"Joseph, I think the people in Dawson are good. I feel safe here. But I see what's going on in the macro community — in the world at large — and I worry about that stuff touching this community. I don't want to be naive. This happened. I can't dismiss

120

this. I can't go home and say, 'Oh, it's just some graffiti.' It's not. It's more than that."

He nods, and then, with a passion I don't expect, he says, "I'll take care of it. I'll get rid of it. I don't want it outside."

In a daze, I leave the store, cross the street, buy my few items at the grocery store, and return home. I don't pass the swastika. I go the opposite way. By the time I tramp through the snow that covers my front walk and enter my house, I find that Musarrat, Pastor Mandy, and Doug have all posted the picture of the swastika on their Facebook pages. Doug posts a long condemnation of whoever carved the symbol into the sidewalk and next to his screed puts a photo of a hundred-dollar bill.

"I will give this bill to anybody who points me in the direction of who did this," he writes. "I'll leave you out of it. Just give me a name. I want a name."

Before long, comments appear on Musarrat's and Mandy's Facebook pages. Together we count more than 140 responses, all positive except one, variations of, "I can't believe this is happening to you guys. I can't believe this kind of hatred still exists." The only negative Facebook post mirrors a comment Doug hears from a Dawson resident who says, referring to me, "Is he going to get all upset whenever something like this happens?"

That afternoon Doug and Joseph dig the swastika out of the sidewalk and pour new concrete into the square. That evening, Doug joins us at our home for dinner. Doug, who has lived in Dawson his entire life and knows everyone in town, says, "I talked to several people who said that it was carved in when the concrete was originally poured."

"I don't buy that," I say. "I take that route every day. I've lived here more than three years. I've walked on that sidewalk a thousand times. And I haven't seen it until today? I'm not that oblivious."

"I'm just reporting what I heard," Doug says. "Not saying I believe it."

"I *don't* believe it."

"Well, about five or six years ago, there was this guy," Doug says, and proceeds to tell us about a clinically disturbed person, possibly schizophrenic, who painted several swastikas on the walls of a building. The people Doug spoke to theorize that he also carved the swastika into the sidewalk.

"I would've seen it," I say.

"My point is," Doug says, "it wasn't directed at you. I do believe that."

"But that's not the point," I say, feeling

my anger rise again. "The point is it's here. It doesn't matter who it was directed to. It is a symbol of hate, of intolerance, of ugliness. Hate should not be here. Hate like this should not exist in the town where I live, fifty feet from my front door."

I sigh, and everyone at our table goes silent, the only sounds in the room our breath and the clatter of silverware on our plates. Finally I say, "Every single person in this town — everyone — should be just as offended by it as I am. What makes me sad . . . and angry . . . is that they aren't."

Doug starts to speak. I cut him off. "Don't tell me to take a breath or cool down. We Muslims can't win. If we keep to ourselves, we're criticized for not blending into society. If we do get engaged, let our voices be heard, we get accused of trying to force in Sharia law or convert people. Either way, we lose."

No one speaks for what seems like thirty seconds, and then my son Imran says in a tiny, barely audible voice, "I want to move."

Musarrat puts her arm around Imran's shoulders and pulls him in to her, holding him, stroking his hair.

That night, I speak with Mandy, who again expresses shock, disgust, and anger. Doug stays for a while after dinner, and I thank him for taking care of the swastika.

"You are a good man," I say to him.

"Thank you," he says.

"I mean that not as an expression but as a definition. You are the definition of a good man."

The next morning, Sunday, after a sleepless night, I swing my feet out of bed, say my prayers, and slowly trudge downstairs. As I come into the living room, I hear a sound coming from outside, a clanging of metal and the crunch and grind of something stabbing into the ground. I peer through our front door and see Jim, our neighbor, shoveling our front walk, just as he does every time it snows. He has never asked us if we want him to shovel our front walk. He just does so on his own, a neighborly gesture, an act of kindness.

*There is so much good here,* I think. *So many good people.*

No, I don't want to leave.

At first I don't think actively about finding an outlet for my anger. It does occur to me that it might be emotionally healthy to channel my anger into something constructive. Or at least look for some means of expressing my anger. But what? I don't have time to take up martial arts. I don't consider myself a viable candidate for therapy, even scream therapy. Running and other forms of exercise do help, briefly, allowing me to blow off steam. But sweating out my anger doesn't seem like enough. Then one day, during one of our appointments, Pastor Mandy asks me if I would consider working with her on an interfaith project she's decided to start. I would give a lecture about my faith, the goal being to dispel myths and correct misconceptions about Muslims.

"Think about it," she says.

*What Islam Is and What It Isn't.*

I do. I talk it over with Musarrat, and finally I come to a decision, the only decision, really. Looking at my life here in Dawson, considering the people I live with and among, it registers that we have an obligation to dispel the myths about Islam, especially now, at this most critical time. We are the only Muslims here, and so, when Pastor Mandy asks me to speak about my faith, I ask myself — is this the right thing to do?

I consider her kindness, her commitment to social justice, her concern about the way minorities are being treated, how they are targeted, especially after the election. I see all that, and I sense her absolute goodness. I believe that I might be able to feed off that — off her goodness. I believe that you can feed off the goodness that surrounds you. Goodness is contagious. You can become inspired to perform an act of goodness just from surrounding yourself with goodness.

"Let's do this," I say to Mandy. "Let's educate. Let's at least try."

I never wanted to give a lecture in Dawson about my faith. My faith is personal, private, not something I really want to share. Yet I feel compelled to do it. I have to do it.

It's the right thing to do.

So here I am.

My struggle.

My jihad.

# 6
## LOGIC AND SINCERITY

A few weeks after the election.

Musarrat, wearing a head scarf, sits at the gate at Dulles International Airport in Virginia, heading back to the Twin Cities after attending the annual Evangelical Lutheran Church in America conference with me and Pastor Mandy.

The election of Donald Trump has brought a wave of feelings that Musarrat hadn't experienced before: discordance, disruption, shock. And then — she's almost sure of it — she feels something else, a disturbing undercurrent, a seismic, pulsating rumble. Something that she knows but doesn't want to accept, not now, not here. Because what she senses coming at her is — hatred.

*I refuse to believe that,* she thinks. *No. I won't believe it.*

She dismisses the feeling, flushes it out of her mind, and determines to embrace only the positive. But after she and I made the decision to stay and I agreed to do the lecture in Dawson, the undercurrent returns. And this time she can't ignore it. It's too loud, too prominent. She feels it, hears it; she sees it played out right in front of her eyes. Not hatred, exactly, she decides. No, not that far. Negativity. Excitability.

"Why do these people feel so threatened?" she asks a friend. "These people know us. They see Ayaz at the clinic. They see me at my salon. Their kids go to school with my kids. What are they so afraid of?"

Abruptly, the myth of Utopia fades.

*I am an outsider,* she thinks, *an outcast.*

And then with a start, she wonders —

*Are these people afraid of me?*

Where am I?

The thoughts buzz inside her head as she scrolls through her cell phone at the airport gate, absently skimming emails, spam, and then — *ping* — she receives a text.

Imran.

Our thirteen-year-old son.

He never texts her.

Unless there is something wrong.

Musarrat looks at the text, reads it once, then leans forward and reads it again, her free hand gripping the arm of the chair in the terminal, her knuckles turning white as bleach.

"Mom," the text reads, "a kid at school called you a part-time suicide bomber."

She rises from her chair, as if ejected from her seat.

"What is it?" I say from the seat next to her.

"Imran."

She calls him and gets the name of the kid. She lets out a tiny gasp. She knows him, she knows the family. The kid, a friend of Imran, has had issues at school. He has been made fun of, he himself has been bullied.

Musarrat tells me about the text and implores me to stay calm. I mutter something about the last straw and bring up Dubai. Musarrat cuts me off. She refuses to discuss leaving Dawson anymore. She says she is calling the school immediately.

She calls the school. The call goes to voice mail. She leaves a message saying that our son has been the victim of racism and she needs to set up a meeting with the principal immediately. Her voice cracking, she explains that she is very upset and this cannot be tolerated. She hangs up, sits back down, and shuts her eyes, absently tapping her phone against her palm. I reach over and gently touch her shoulder. She nods, opens her eyes, smiles at me, then calls Imran back to gauge how he feels. He seems, well, like *Imran* — cool, together, sweet. This calms her down. She realizes that the school is heading into the weekend and that the principal won't be able to meet us until Monday at the earliest.

She hangs up with Imran after promising to check in regularly.

"When will it get easier?" she asks me.

I shake my head and put my arm around her.

The following week, Musarrat and I meet with the principal, a teacher's aide, and a school social worker. Everyone agrees that what the kid said to Imran was unacceptable. Musarrat has thought a lot about the incident over the weekend and insists that the school not involve the kid's parents.

"It's so unfortunate," someone says, "but we hear about this type of thing a lot. It happens all the time."

Musarrat feels her cheeks burn.

"It *shouldn't* happen all the time," she says. "It is not okay. Kids have to learn how hurtful this is and how wrong. This cannot become the norm."

By the end of the meeting, we feel that

the school has truly heard us and will take steps to condemn such behavior in the future. We're not sure if the principal will schedule a school assembly to talk about the incident or if teachers will be asked to discuss the incident in their classes. Musarrat does hear that at a school concert a few days later, Imran chooses to sit next to the kid who called her a suicide bomber.

*I've dealt with this one horrible moment involving my son,* she thinks. *But I can't stop them from hating us.*

"You've got an hour," Mandy tells me. "That's it. Then I think you should take some questions."

One hour.

I know comparative religions well. It's a hobby of sorts, but in this case, I can't allow myself to speak off the cuff. I will have to prepare. I want the audience to understand, to process the information I present. There is so much information. The media spews so much misinformation. I need to correct that. But do I have enough time? Where do I start? Can I get everything in?

One hour.

"This has to be good," I say aloud, pacing upstairs in my office late at night, the rest of the household asleep for hours. Mandy has heard through the grapevine that hundreds of people may attend the lecture.

*It has to be really good,* I think. *Because I'm never going to do this again.*

"I will tell people what Islam is," I murmur, thinking aloud. "The reality. I need to distinguish the reality from the falsehoods. This is what you're told. The lies. Now here is the truth. Here are the facts. Here is logic. Here is sincerity. I'm telling you the *truth.*"

I decide that I will start with the insanity spread by certain media — and now our government — that all Muslims are terrorists. I will counter that claim by pointing out Christian terrorists such as the Lord's Resistance Army in Africa, which has killed a hundred thousand people in the name of Christ. I will reference Jim Jones, the KKK, Dylann Roof. Those are all terrorists, but nobody brands them by that term. Yet *all* Muslims are called that, just because they're Muslim. That's not logical. That's not right.

"Logic and sincerity," I say, pacing, nodding, and then I stop to scribble notes on a yellow legal pad. "Heart and mind. I am giving this town direct access to a practicing Muslim."

I freeze, nod to an invisible audience.

"You've probably never met somebody like me before," I say, trying it out.

I have no margin for error. None. Zero. I'm a brown Muslim person defending my faith.

People often spout certain so-called facts or common beliefs, and when asked about their source, they say, "Well, I read that somewhere, or I heard this . . ."

I can't do that. I have to give the exact source, the time period, the context. I have to give everything.

*You can do nothing wrong, Ayaz. Because if you do, you'll be crucified.*

I shake my head.

I have to know their religion better than they do. I have to know my religion better than most Muslims do.

I sit at my desk, my leg pumping, and I began picking out passages and jotting notes. As I write, I suddenly realize that, incredibly, some people will come to my lecture because they want to convert *me*. They want to save me. They believe that the only way I can be saved is if I become a Christian. Otherwise, I'm going to Hell. I've actually heard that expressed. Mandy told me that someone she knows, a patient of mine, said to her, "I like him, he's a great doctor, but unfortunately, he's the anti-Christ, and he's going to Hell."

It's ludicrous.

But I cannot get angry. I cannot feed into anyone's fear.

I remember a teaching from the Gospels about being saved. I riffle through my Bible to find it, recalling it as I flip pages —

On Judgment Day, Jesus will say, "Many of you called me Lord, praised and worshipped me. You cast out demons in my name. But you will never make it to salvation. You will be gnashing your teeth on the gates and I will turn you away because you are wicked people."

Jesus says this because the road that leads to salvation is narrow and very few find it. The road to destruction, on the other hand, is wide. Most people end up walking down that road.

"Okay," I say, "let's say two hundred people attend the lecture. Jesus said, 'Few find their way to salvation.' How do you define *few*? Is it ten percent? Fifteen percent? Let's be generous and say twenty percent. That means only forty people of my imagined two hundred audience members will be saved. The others will go to Hell. So which forty people? Which ones?"

Bottom line: according to the Bible, I may not be saved, but neither will you.

In the days leading up to the lecture, I

spend at least thirty hours preparing. I do almost all the writing and research at night, after everyone's asleep. I pace, I speak aloud, I rush to my desk and scribble thoughts, phrases, and passages, and then finally I organize everything and write the lecture out by hand on a yellow legal pad, creating a sprawling fifteen-page outline. I then type everything into my computer and print it out. The night before the lecture, I invite Musarrat and Mandy to listen to me deliver it in my dining room. I'm wearing scrubs, so it's not exactly a dress rehearsal, but I stand at one side of the table as Musarrat and Mandy take their seats across from me.

"I'm not going to do the entire lecture," I say. "Just a synopsis."

"Great," Musarrat says.

"I'll just give you the key points, so you can get the idea."

"Sounds good," Mandy says.

"I didn't think you'd want to sit through the whole thing —"

"Ayaz," Musarrat says. "Just do it."

"Right. You're right. Okay. Here goes. All right, introduction, yadda yadda yadda, welcome, thank you very much, *so.*"

I exhale and launch into my lecture. I read from my printed pages, my head down, my eyes glued on my notes.

After a few minutes, I hear movement from across the table — Musarrat and Mandy crossing their legs, clearing their throats, changing positions. I skip a few points in my outline, realize that a couple of thoughts may be repetitive, and quickly power through to the end.

I look up and grin. "Well, that's the gist. And yeah, I know I sort of raced through everything, especially some of the historical stuff and the philosophy and the comparative religion points, but I'll deliver it more forcefully tomorrow night, and I'll slow down, and I'll make better eye contact, that goes without saying. So, okay, what did you think? Be honest."

Musarrat and Mandy stare at me with the same exact expression. Their jaws hang open, their faces have gone pale, and their pupils seem dilated. I can't exactly read those looks. I'm guessing they are stunned or, maybe, amazed. Neither speaks for a good twenty seconds.

Finally, Musarrat says, "What *was* that?"

"That was my, ah, you know, lecture."

"No," Musarrat says. "It isn't."

"No," Mandy says. "You can't. This is not going to work."

"You mean?" I frown. "What do you mean?"

"I know this stuff," Mandy says. "And I didn't understand half of what you said."

I fight back a sudden feeling of panic.

"I worked on this for a long time. Hours and hours. I want to educate them."

"Definitely," Musarrat says.

"Absolutely," Mandy says.

I squint at them. "So —"

"You need to rethink this," Mandy says.

"The whole thing?"

"The entire thing," Mandy says.

"These people don't understand Islam," Musarrat says. "They know nothing."

"Zero," Mandy says.

"You have to start with the basics," Musarrat says.

"You have to pretend you're talking to fourth graders," Mandy says.

"Seriously?"

"Yes," Mandy says, eyeing my outline. "This is not what they want."

"Oh." I frown again. "What do they want?"

Mandy holds up her hand and extends three fingers.

"Three things," she says, ticking off one finger at a time. "Terrorism. Sharia law. Women."

"One more thing," Musarrat says. "They have to know that we're not trying to convert them."

"Right, four things," Mandy says. "I'll say something about that in my introduction, but you should mention it as well."

I look at the outline now bunched up in my hands. "You didn't like the part where I talked about the philosophical significance of —"

"NO," Mandy and Musarrat say together.

"Terrorism, Sharia, women," I say, and then mumble the words again. I look across the table at those two smart, kind, extremely powerful women, and I smile with a sudden jolt of knowledge.

"You know what, you two?" I say. "You're right. Excuse me."

I spin out of the dining room and charge up to my second-floor office, taking the stairs two at a time. I grab a fresh blank legal pad and furiously begin writing. Four hours later, starting from square one, I've written a brand-new eleven-page outline, start to finish, focusing on terrorism, Sharia law, and women. It is the lecture I present now.

# 7
# FAITH IS WHAT YOU DO

"Let's talk about terrorism."

I slowly exhale, sip some water, and listen as the word echoes through the auditorium. I can feel its impact land. I nod and say a silent thank-you to Musarrat and Mandy for being honest about my terrible first draft. Without them, I would've died out here.

"One purpose I have tonight is for all of you to understand that the 0.01 percent of Muslims that you see on TV are not my spokespeople. They are not the spokespeople for my religion. Somewhere between 9/11 and now, a bait and switch happened, where all of a sudden you have been exposed to religious doctrine and teachings from the *media* — not from scholars, not from people like me."

I catch myself.

*Do I sound arrogant?*

I hear rustling in the dark. I sense —

139

something. A tensing. A ripple of unease, of doubt, of discomfort. I don't mind challenging the audience; I just don't want to lose them. And I don't want to come across as condescending in any way. Then a lightbulb flickers on in my mind, illuminates me. *I'm not teaching. I'm explaining.* I need to find more common ground, more humility.

But I feel my conviction rising into my throat again. I can't help myself. I speak through what has become a consistent burning in my throat.

"You know who does that? Bill Maher. That's what he does. Now, Bill Maher is a funny comedian. He does political analysis. But he doesn't know anything about Islam. He presents one side only. When he talks about Christianity, I know better than that. It doesn't faze me. So, I would ask for the same standard when you look at me, *the same standard.*"

I know I've gone way off my outline. I don't dare look at Musarrat. I can almost feel her shooting a laser gaze at me. *Ayaz, where are you going with this? Come back. Focus.*

But I have to say this. I have to go there. *I will wind my way back to my outline,* I silently promise.

"It's so easy to go there because Satan

140

comes to us at all angles. In the Quran it says he comes to you from the right, he comes to you from the left, he comes to you from the front, he comes to you from the back. He is ready. He is the deceiver. We should all be mindful. I'm not worried, though, because there is going to be a Day of Judgment. Every one of us will have to account for our sins, including me. I am not worried about anyone else. I am worried about myself. There is always justice. You cannot escape that."

I pause. I plant my feet, face forward, not seeing but imagining the audience before me, barely stirring, their attention rapt.

"Okay," I say. "So, we have defined a purpose for tonight."

I hold for a longer pause now, mostly to ease my raging throat.

*We want to know one another,*" I say, the emphasis surprising me.

I spread my arms wide, as if presenting myself to this audience as an offering. After a moment, I drop my arms to my side. "So how do we get there? How do we get to that purpose? The only way is devotion to knowledge, devotion to wisdom. We have to put in effort in order to learn."

I stand in the middle of the stage, gripping the sides of the podium.

"Love thy neighbor," I whisper.

That is tonight's premise. That is tonight's purpose. My purpose.

"Why am I here?" I ask. After a pause, I answer, "To know my Lord."

I let the words land.

"What is the equation for that, for knowing your Lord?" I say. I circle a phrase in my outline with my fingertip. "Well, according to Islam, the equation begins with the idea that *bad deeds stain.*"

Now, tapping the page in front of me, I rattle off each part of the equation: "When your soul is stained, it puts distance between you and God. Where there is distance, you can't know your God. When you can't know your God, you can't love your God. If you can't love your God, then you are lost."

My rapid-fire point-by-point breakdown leaves me momentarily breathless. I pause to gather myself. I exhale slowly, a kind of cleansing breath I've learned not from yoga but from daily prayer.

"You know, sometimes when I wash my hands, I'll look at the water. Just look at the water. It's amazing. This clear stuff — seventy percent of it is me. It's you. The stamp of the Creator is all around us."

I drop my hands and turn to the next page in my outline. I nod at the word at the top of the page, a word I have underlined in bold.

**_Knowledge._**

"It says in the Quran that it is incumbent upon every Muslim, male and female, to seek knowledge from the cradle to the grave. From when you're born until you die. Because that knowledge — that wisdom — will save you."

I pause because I want to listen to the audience.

*Are they hearing me?*

*Am I connecting?*

I want these people, almost all of whom I cannot see, to know me, to know who I am, to know what I believe.

*Give me that,* I say silently. *Hear me.*

*Know me.*

I want my neighbors to know me.

"Knowledge," I repeat. "It's far more important than any type of ritual worship. Some people have the idea that worship is going to church and that's it. It's important, sure, but that's not the game. That's not life. I look at life this way: Life is like the Indy 500. Five hundred laps. Five hundred laps with pit stops. You've got to tune up, change the tires, recharge the battery. That's *church.*"

The audience reacts. Laughter, rustling,

and maybe even applause from a few people. I smile and keep going.

"Life is right now. Your religion is right now. What do you *do*? Your actions. If you took the time to learn, that's good. Actions. How do you treat your brother or your sister? Do you give from your heart? Do you smile? Even a smile can be charity. How did I treat my patient the other day? Did I do the right thing? When I got called on the weekend at two in the morning, did I respond the right way?"

I hear a hush. The audience can sense that I am about to share something intimate.

"I'm telling you this because I'm not perfect. I have to constantly work on it — work on myself. When I get upset, I ask myself, Why? Why do I feel this way? Who am I? *Who am I?* What is my purpose? Where am I going?"

I lower my voice so I am whispering into the microphone.

"It's like a switch," I say. "I then step back and I say, 'Oh, my God. This is my honor. How could I even feel frustrated that I have to get up, even at two in the morning?' It is my *honor* to treat this individual who is suffering. It is. That's how I do it. This is it. This is my equation. It is not an easy road. It's a lot easier to have other people tell you

144

what to think."

I remember a few of the insensitive, inaccurate, uneducated comments people have made to me and about me.

People who may be here, in this audience, I think.

"Is he a citizen?" someone asked Doug recently.

"Yes," Doug said. "He is a citizen of Dawson."

"But is he a citizen of the United States?"

And the day after the election, a woman approached me, offering me a beatific smile, her face practically glowing.

"Jesus loves you," she said.

I smiled back, and maybe even mumbled, "Thank you." But as I walked away, I wondered what she would have said if I'd answered her, "Muhammad loves you."

"Knowledge," I say, leaning into the mic with my elbows on the podium. "It is not an easy road. We are so gullible. So easily swayed. We wait for the pundits to tell us what to think so that we can tell everybody else what *we* think when we really didn't come up with those ideas ourselves. That's the low road."

I shuffle through my outline and quickly find the quote I'm looking for. I point at it and say, "Jesus tells us in the Gospel of Matthew 7:13–14, 'Enter through the narrow gate for broad is the gate that leads to Hell, and many may enter through it. But small is the gate and narrow is the road that leads to Heaven and life, and only few find it.' "

I look up, squint, and say, "That's not the Quran. That is the Gospel. Jesus is telling you and me that all of us in this room, many of us are taking the low road. *Many of us,* including me. That's why I want people to tell me when I am wrong because the next time I will speak more accurately. I have to account for my deeds. I have to account for my deeds, because when I die, I want to be in front of my Lord who is going to say, 'Did you?' and I am going to say, 'I did,' and He is going to say, 'Hey, enter.' "

The crowd stirs. I can't tell if they find this presentation of God amusing, insightful, or offensive. I do know I have their attention.

I spread my arms slightly and shrug. "There's no need for words, right? He knows you already. He already knows you. He knows us."

I turn my head, cough, and then focus on my voice booming through the auditorium, feeling strangely disconnected from it, as if the voice belongs to someone else. "Whatever you hear, *think.* Be skeptical. We should all be open-minded but be skeptical. Otherwise we fall into traps."

I open my eyes, squint at my notes, and read, "The Quran says, 'Oh, mankind, we indeed created you from male and female and made you into many nations and tribes so that you may know one another. Indeed, the most noble of you in the sight of God is the most righteous of you.' "

I look up and absently slap the pages of my outline. "This is the *Quran,* okay? It doesn't say that the most noble is the one who is a Muslim. It doesn't say that the most noble is the one who sits there and prays all day. Righteousness, good deeds, good heart. Prayer."

*Prayer.*

I pray — five times a day, every day.

At home before sunrise, then twice at work, and again at home after work, usually right before dinner, and finally at night.

Each prayer takes between five and ten minutes.

At the hospital, I keep a prayer rug in my office. I will try to fit in my prayers either during lunchtime or when I have a few minutes between patients. I begin with ablution, or washing at the sink, a symbolic purification we call *wudu.* I wash my nose, mouth, ears, hands, and forearms, three times each. It's a baptism of sorts, but whereas Christians undergo a single baptism in the course of their lives, we have a baptism every day. After I perform wudu, I go into my office and lock the door. My coworkers and staff know that I'm praying and give me the time, respect, and quiet I need.

In the office, I pull the visitor's chair to one side, giving myself enough space to kneel and enabling me to face east, toward Mecca. I turn the lights off, unroll my prayer rug, kneel down on it, bow my head, close my eyes, and complete the prayers. When I finish, I stand, fold up the prayer rug, hit the lights, and get back to work.

I say essentially the same prayers every day, texts from the Quran, some verses I have memorized, some I read aloud, all of which I recite slowly. In Islam, we believe that the prayer begins when it ends — with the deeds you perform after the prayer is done. The ritual is meant as a reaffirmation of our faith. Nothing more. It's a kind of check-in. We ask of ourselves, "What are you doing? How are you treating people? Are you doing the right thing? What are you doing when nobody is watching?"

By praying and holding myself up to these

standards every day, five times a day, I am exercising discipline. Beyond the philosophy of my religion, or any religion, we begin, I believe, with just that: discipline. The routine, the repetition, the discipline ground you, and that, in turn, provides you a measure of humility, of humanity.

As part of human nature, we always want more. We never have enough. We want more success, more money, more possessions. We seek more compliments, more affirmation, more adulation. We have a problem feeling simply satisfied. We want something new; we want *more.* We actually find, in neuro-psychiatric literature, that novelty in the brain stimulates neurons, which are more powerful even than our neurons associated with love. The desire for *more* affects us mentally. It's chemical. We can't help ourselves. But the discipline of praying several times a day counteracts that. I believe that because I see the ritual of prayer as a disciplinary action. That is the key word: *action.* Prayer is an action.

I also see a distinction between prayer and worship.

Worship is what you give to God; prayer is what you ask of God.

I believe that God taught Muhammad how to pray and that he in turn taught his followers how to pray.

It begins with the reminder of this seemingly contradictory statement: there is no God but God. *La Ilaha Ilallah.*

I have always found that sentiment to be so beautiful and so powerful. The statement begins in the negative — *There is no God* — and moves into the positive — *There is nothing but God.*

The statement *Allahu akbar* has been often misinterpreted. It doesn't mean that God is great. It means that God is *greater.* The phrase is a comparative, not a superlative. It suggests that God is greater than anything we as human beings can possibly imagine. God exists in the absolute world. We exist in the relative world. How do you process the absolute world? You can't. There is no way to understand it. We understand a relative world because we see comparatives every day — tall, short, heavy, thin, smart, not smart. God doesn't exist in that realm. God is the absolute — the all-knowing. It would be like trying to process the concept of infinity. We recognize the symbol for the term, but we don't know what it really means.

This is very much inherent in the Islamic faith. We know the existence of God, but we don't have an image for what God is. We don't believe that God is a wise-looking old man with a white beard, sitting on a throne. We don't believe that God has a gender. We don't know if God is a he or a she. We know only that God is the all-merciful, the most beneficent, the all-loving. The Divine is trust, the Divine is love, the Divine is kindness.

God is the one and only judge. We humans — we Muslims — are so fallible, so imperfect; we can be so wrong. I see that in myself. I am so fallible. But we make choices and those choices should be to try to emulate the qualities of the Creator — generosity, love, virtue, dignity, sincerity.

Again, *actions*.

To pray is to *act*.

And I believe that prayer — sincere prayer — works.

But not without action. Never without action.

Martin Luther King, Jr., once said that we can't just pray, we have to work. We have to use our logic, our minds. He didn't dismiss the value of prayer. But he insisted that we can't *just* pray. I've taken Dr. King's words to heart and I try to live by this credo: work as though everything depends on you, and pray as though everything depends on God.

We Muslims are told to pray — but also

not to *overpray.* I remember a story about a man who went to the mosque every day to pray. He never missed a day. A prophet came in one day, saw the guy, and asked, "Who is that?"

"Oh, he's trying to be better than you," someone answered. "He's trying to pray even more than you do."

The prophet said, "Who is feeding his family?"

The man answered, "The community does. We support him."

The prophet said, "He is not closer to God than you are. God doesn't tell you to sit there and worship all day. It says in Islam, 'The ink of a scholar is holier than the blood of a martyr. The sleep of a wise person is better than an ignorant person up all night praying.' "

Prayer.

It begins when it ends.

God gave me a brain, God gave me a heart. When I read, when I work, when I think, when I perform a good deed, when I love — all of these actions, that's prayer.

The Bible, James 2:26, says, "Faith without deeds" is nothing.

Faith is a verb, not a noun.

Faith is what you do.

■ ■ ■ ■

"All right," I say to the audience. "Now we're going to get into an exercise to prove that none of us is as smart as we think. Should I skip it?"

A few people laugh, and I feel myself grin.

"I'm just kidding. So I'm going to read you a quote, and you are going to tell me if it's from the Bible or the Quran, okay?"

I look up and say, intending to be disarming, "I want the protestors to answer. I welcome you. All right? Ready? Let's start with a simple one. You don't have to tell me which Gospel or chapter, nothing like that. Just say which of the two books, the Quran or the Bible. Okay?"

I begin to read the first quote, my finger tracking the words beneath the line, "And Jesus sensed this belief in them. He said, 'Who are my helpers unto God?' The apostles said, 'We are God's helpers. We believe in God and bear witness we are submitters.' "

I raise my head and feel a new surge of energy crackling through the room.

"How many say this is from the Bible? Raise your hands."

I hear rustling, murmuring, but I see

153

no hands.

"I'll read it again," I say. When I finish, I say, "Come on. Be brave. What's in your heart? How many say this is from the Bible?"

I shield my face with my hand so I can make out the first few rows of the audience. I hear hesitation, nervous laughter, and then many of the audience members shoot their hands in the air.

"Okay. Most of you." I pause. "This is the Quran, chapter three, verse fifty-two."

A rush of sound erupts — a stew of confusion, embarrassed laughter, rumbling as people move in their seats, some outright giggles and voices cascading over each other.

"Okay. Next verse: 'On account of the angels, a woman should have a covering over her head to show she is under her husband's authority.'"

Silence.

"How many believe this is from the Quran?" I say, speaking too loudly, scorching my throat. "Come on. Be brave. Must be the Quran, right? Come on. Raise your hands."

Again, many people raise their hands.

I shake my head. "No. This is First Corinthians. The Bible."

I hold, again taking in the sound of the

154

audience, another mix of disbelief, surprise, and even some embarrassed laughter.

"Next quote. Ready? The angels said, 'Oh, Mary, truly God gives thee glad tiding of a word from Him whose name is the Messiah Jesus, son of Mary, high honored in this world and in the hereafter.' She said, 'Oh, Lord, how will I have a child while no man has touched me?' He said, 'Thus did God create whatever He wills.' "

I trace the last line and speak softly into the microphone.

"How many believe this is from the Bible?"

I hear some people murmuring, questioning each other, but this time I don't wait for an answer or a show of hands.

"It's from the Quran, chapter three, verse forty-five. I want the protestors to talk to me about this one afterwards. Please. Set me straight. Teach me. Please."

I sense people in the audience sliding forward in their seats. They have become completely engaged in "the Bible or the Quran?" exercise. I hear them whispering to each other, anticipating the next verse.

"Next one," I say. "You ready?"

A hum of assent.

I read, "Say, all my servants who have transgressed against their souls, despair not of the mercy of God. God forgives all sins. Indeed, it is He who is forgiving the merciful."

I raise my eyes, catch a whole row of confused faces, their foreheads creased in thought.

"How many believe this is from the Bible?"

Several hands shoot up. After a few seconds, others raise their hands tentatively, allowing their fingers only to reach as high as their ears.

"It's the Quran," I say, and then I press on, feeling my throat burn. "So to those who think that this God of Islam is saying, 'Go behead people, go kill people, go oppress women,' *no*. Saying this is anathema to what the Quran stands for. Right? Does that make any sense?"

I wait. I shake my head slowly.

"Next quote," I say, and read, "For God loved the world so much that He gave His only son so that all who believe in Him may not die but have everlasting life." I squint into the lights. "How many believe that is from the Bible?

A flurry of hands waving, voices rising. I see not a tentative, hesitant hand anywhere.

"Are you sure?" I say.

A small titter of laughter.

"Okay, you're right. John 3:16. Beautiful passage. *Beautiful* passage. I mean, it shows the mercy of God. Oh, my gosh. He gave His only son. That is a God who is worth worshipping. All right. Final one. Ready?"

I stare at this quote for a count of three, and then my voice rises, rages, as I read, "If your right hand causes you to sin, cut it off and throw it away. It is much better for you to lose one of your limbs than your whole body to go to Hell."

I stop abruptly and whisper into the microphone, "How many think this is from the Quran?"

A slew of hands, fingers flapping, folks eager, sure.

"So, no, it's from the Bible."

Silence.

"Matthew," I say. "Not just from the Bible, this is the Gospel. This is Jesus telling you this. *Jesus.* I thought Islam was the one that lopped off limbs. Right?"

*Let them hear this,* I think. *Let these words penetrate.*

Let them understand.

"Again, we have to consider *context,*" I say, my voice cracking, sore, weary. "I could read this, and a bunch of zealots could go start cutting people, but that would not be Christianity because you have to take these things along with the entire life of Jesus and understand that He was a . . . a . . ."

I stumble because I am speaking too fast, too purposefully, too passionately. I quickly autocorrect.

"He is trying to get you to go to *Heaven*," I say. "He is telling you this so you can go and do the right thing. That's what this is about. He's saying, do the right thing, which is the same thing we are told in Islam. The same thing."

I clear my throat. I shouldn't. I can't help myself. My throat roars in flame. I cough.

"The exercise is over," I croak. "We're moving on. The fun part is over."

# 8
## "ISLAM SUPPORTS TERRORISM"

"I want to hit the misconceptions directly," I say. And then I say, emphasizing the word: "Terrorism."

I pause. Something new pulses from the audience, an emotion I can't quite identify.

Discomfort?

No.

More like defiance.

"I've read the Bible many times. I've read the Quran many times. I've read scholars talking about these works because, honestly, some of this stuff is out of my realm. I don't understand it."

I hear a muted reaction to my confession.

"I have to rely on scholars. Professor John Voll from Georgetown University, for example, whom I mentioned. What does he say? What does he mean? What is the context? There is no shame in wondering that. We can't understand everything. I certainly can't."

I shuffle the pages on the podium and I read, glancing briefly into the lights, "The Quran. It is said that each verse has between seven and seventy *thousand* meanings."

The audience murmurs.

I nod. "I know. Sometimes I can't even get one . . . or two. Maybe. *Maybe.*"

I slap the podium.

*Here we go,* I think. *It's on.*

"Misconception number one: Islam supports and promotes terrorism."

I look up so quickly that the pages in front of me flutter and nearly fly off the podium.

"How many people believe that? Be honest. Nothing wrong with being honest. How many people believe that?"

I peer into the audience, the lights again causing me to squint. I see no hands.

"You see it on the news all the time. You see these zealots. *Islam supports terrorism.* How many people believe that?"

I shield my eyes with my hands.

"Where are the brave ones? Where are you?"

*You protested this talk,* I think. *Come on. I know you're here. Show yourselves.*

Still, I see no hands. Not one. Zero.

I rap my fist on the podium. "That statement is absolutely false, categorically, in every way. I condemn it. Period. *Period.*"

I point at the evidence, the quotes I've written down, the research I've pulled not from a hasty Google search but from books, works by respected scholars.

"Islam says yes, you may fight — in *wars*. But only in wars of self-defense. And only in wars where you are defending somebody else. Think of when someone finally stands up to the bully at school. Islam is telling you, *you have to defend that guy.* If you don't, *you are not a Muslim.*"

I pause. In a brief instant, in a flash, I picture Imran at school. I see him walking down the hallway, flanked by rows of lockers, and I hear that kid, his so-called friend, calling his mom — Musarrat — a suicide bomber. The image melts into a sour, rotten taste that lingers in my mouth and then snags inside my throat. I want to spit the image out.

And then Pastor Mandy's face pops into view, filling my field of vision. I blink furiously. I have conjured her, I must have, because I don't actually *see* her. All I can make out is a bunch of silver backlit shapes, silhouettes. But Pastor Mandy appears clearly, her face full and defined. She is smiling, her eyes half closed as she nods in agreement. She knows what lies ahead — the core of the lecture.

I say, "Muhammad said the person who doesn't want for his neighbor what he wants for himself has no faith. Jesus said love thy neighbor. Love everyone the way I love them."

My voice rises, hits a higher pitch, then whirs into a plea. "Where is the difference there? What is the difference between Islam and Christianity? Who cares who actually said it, Muhammad or Jesus? The message is the same. *Love thy neighbor.* The Quran says in verse 4:74, 'What ails you that you do not fight in the way of God for the weak and the oppressed men, women, and children who cry out, "Lord, give us a protector, a helper"? Those who believe fight in the way of God and fight against the allies of Satan. Satan is ever feeble.' "

I look up and say, "Now context, right? When this verse was created, it was after Muhammad fled from Mecca to Medina because he was being persecuted. A bunch of people — innocent people — were left behind. The Meccans, the pagans, routinely tortured and butchered children. They cut off their hands, their arms . . . this was routine. The Quran is saying, 'Go back and help them. Fight for them. But fight in the way of your Lord.' What does that mean? Muhammad says, 'Fight only those who fight you. Do not kill women. Do not kill children. Do not kill the elderly. And if those you fight stop, then you stop. Because God does not love the starter of wars.' "

Silence. Once again, I feel as if I've hit a communal nerve.

*They've never heard anything like this before,* I think.

Then I hear Pastor Mandy's words in my head —

*This is the first time anyone like you has ever spoken to them.*

I peer into the audience. "So you say that terrorists are killing people in the name of Islam, right? Come on. You see that all the time."

I feel my voice rise and try to tamp it down. "That's the *0.01 percent* that I told you about. Again, they don't represent me. I would remind you as I remind myself, in the Gospel of Matthew 10:34, Jesus says, 'I come not to bring the peace but to bring the sword.' Or in Ezekiel 9:6, God said, 'Go through the city and kill. Spare no one. Have no mercy.' That's *Ezekiel.*"

I read rapidly, punching the words, " 'Kill the old man. Kill the young man. Kill the women. Kill the mothers and the children. Defile the temple and fill its courtyards with corpses.' That's the *Bible.* "

163

I raise my head and flatten my palm onto the page before me. "This was during the Babylonian time, when the Jews were exiled and the Jews of Babylon were misbehaving and Ezekiel was the prophet, saying, 'Listen, we've got to do something about this, okay?' "

I drop my voice. "Now. Imagine if I take these few verses and I go on a news station and I show pictures of the KKK, and I show pictures of the IRA — Irish Republican Army — and I show pictures of the things that have happened with Islamophobia in this country, and believe me, I travel a lot. People are scared. Good people in other countries are scared."

I tap the side of my head.

*"Think."*

I pause.

"It's wrong to suggest that only Muslims are terrorists and they are killing Christians. Killing Christians and Westerners. To say that it's a war of religions. It's us versus them. Right? Come on. *Right?*"

I shake my head slowly. "On the Day of Judgment, you can't hide what's been in your heart. You might fool yourself and you might fool me, but you can't fool somebody else where it counts, right?"

I look off now, my mind racing. I disappear into my head, and I say, almost dreamily, "We live eighty years, seventy years, fifty years, and then what happens? This world *ends.*"

I shut my eyes, nod, and feel myself swaying slightly.

"I'm going to break for a moment. I want to explain what is, in the Islamic context, an illusion. But this is important, so allow me to explain it. And then I will prove something to you."

I open my eyes, smile, and say, "We have two essences: an animal essence, which is where we live here, and a spiritual essence, which lives throughout eternity. Think about it this way. We have infinity, right? Take a number of years, years of life. Say you live fifty years or eighty years or even just ten years. Take eighty years, as an example. What is eighty divided by infinity? Zero. What's fifty divided by infinity? Zero. What is one second divided by infinity? Zero. Anything — any number — divided by infinity is zero. That is a fact. But this is important."

I hold, I breathe. I know I'm breaking my promise to Musarrat and Mandy to stick to my three topics, terrorism, women, and Sharia, but this is important, this is crucial, so I press on —

"All of it is *zero*. Zero means nothing, you are not here. This is an important illusion, because infinity is where we are going, right? Now, it's either a positive infinity or a negative infinity. It's either Heaven or Hell, right? So your actions actually matter. Your actions play a critical role in determining which infinity you're going to. Jesus knew this because He said the kingdom of God is at hand. He said, 'It's coming. It's here.' And people use this to discredit Him and say, *Well, He died and it's not here, therefore He was wrong.* But He knew that this — that *this* —"

I wave my hand at the audience, at the auditorium, at this space.

"— is nothing."

I speak now as if I'm being timed to see how rapid-fire I can blast out the words. "When infinity is the denominator, the answer is always zero. So when Jesus says the kingdom of God is near, it could be five years, it could be a hundred, it could be a million, it could be *a billion years.* It's the same, right? We cannot grasp the infinite. Again, again . . . our actions right now are all that matter."

I don't know if I've lost the crowd, but I know I have to bring myself back to my notes, to the topic of terrorism. I hear the ticking of an imaginary clock. Suddenly this lecture, these words appear to expand in scope, in significance. This feels so important to me, so very, very important.

*I need to get through to them,* I think.

I rustle through my pages on the podium and find my place.

"Okay, the facts," I say. "Here we go with the facts again. Ninety-four percent of terrorist attacks performed in the United States from 1980 to 2005 were committed by non-Muslims. Ninety-four percent. This comes from the Department of Justice. You can go to their website and check it out. Don't go to the media. Go to them. Please look it up if you don't believe me. I have nothing to prove to anybody. I am only interested in the truth. I am here because I need to be here, not because I want to talk about my religion. I seriously *don't.*"

I don't. I really don't.

"This is personal," I say, and bite my lip. I am allowing these people in the audience — my neighbors — to see me in a way I seldom allow myself to be seen.

"I really didn't want to do this," I say. "But I think I need to. I need to be here."

I scan my outline, begin to read the statistics, the facts.

"Listen to this. According to the State

Department . . . now, this is the Country Report on Terrorism. Under the US Statute, Title 22, Sections 26-56F — the State Department by law must report to Congress every year on terrorism, by *law*."

I swallow as I stare at the statistics before me. These statistics hurt. They pain me as I read them.

"In 2015, ISIS killed fourteen people in San Bernardino, California, and then, how many at Pulse, in the nightclub in Florida? Fifty, I think, something like that. That was in 2016, so it didn't make it into this particular report. So we'll say, we'll estimate, sixty to seventy-five, total. In 2015, there were 130 people killed in Paris. Let's say two hundred to simplify the numbers. In 2015, they killed 7,500 Iraqi Muslims. In 2014, they killed *twelve thousand* Iraqi Muslims. Brown people like me. You don't hear this because you see the news through a certain . . . eye. But when I travel — I do a lot of traveling — I watch American news, I watch Arab news, I watch Canadian news, I watch Iranian news, I watch Russian news. I look at it all because I want to see all the biases. I am looking for a central point. I am looking for the truth."

I speak now in a hush. "Did you know there were imams — Muslim priests, Muslim pastors in Iraq — who condemned ISIS and then got beheaded the next day? People who condemn ISIS are killed. Slaughtered. That's real. That's palpable to me. That's visceral. I feel it in my heart."

The audience before me comes to life. I hear a chorus of murmuring, throat clearing, and . . . I think I hear . . . sniffling.

I pause.

"It shouldn't even matter," I say wearily. "We should care that people are dying. People. Just people . . . who breathe, who have a heartbeat. Anybody. And who cares if they're gay or if they're black or white or if they're Muslim? It's a person. God made them. Like you. You're no better than that person. I am no better than that person."

I flip quickly to a quote I've been saving. "Imam Ali, one of the successors of the Prophet, said, 'You must go to every person as if they're better than you. You have to look at them as though they are better than you, and if you don't, you are not a Muslim.' "

I sniff and say slowly, "I practice that. That's real to me. When I see a patient, I look at him or her, and I say, it's true, I say, 'You're better than me.' I say that. I mean that."

I look up now, and my eyes feel adjusted

to the glare of the lights because I see the mass of faces in front of me. They look at me raptly, their eyes riveted into mine.

*How can people who don't know me hate me?*

"I've been blessed," I whisper. "I had a family that took care of me. I had the opportunity to go to college and to medical school. My family has given me so much. If I were put in a different position, maybe I would have been a bad person. That's very, very possible. I hope not, but I don't know. I believe that we have to live our blessings."

I'm veering off topic again. Getting too personal.

"Now, that math, again the math. By the way, those twenty thousand Iraqis, that doesn't include everything. That doesn't include rape. That doesn't include slavery. Let me read this part to you."

I glance down at the information I've printed out, and I say, almost from memory, "In 2015, ISIL abducted, systematically raped, and abused thousands of women and children, some as young as eight."

I shake my head. "My daughter is nine. It burns to read this. Women and children are being sold and enslaved, sold as spoils of war, forced into marriage and servitude, and we don't want *refugees*? We want to stop them from coming here? I saw someone say on Fox News, 'Oh, these refugees, how dare they come here? Why don't they just fight? And if they're not willing to fight, then they must be terrorists.' These people? What are they supposed to fight with? A fork and a knife? They don't have guns. They are workers or plumbers or carpenters or farmers or doctors or . . . whatever. They don't have anything. They're mothers and children and babies. We don't want them? Oh, no. We don't want you here. Is that Jesus? Is that what this country wants to be?

"Only half of one percent of the world's refugee population comes here. One half of one percent. We are the richest nation in the world. We have the biggest army in the world. We spend more on our military than the next ten countries combined. And we refuse refugees? We shut them out? We refuse orphans? What kind of message is that? Is that what America is about?"

# 9
# HER CHOICE, NOT MINE

Washington, DC.

Pastor Mandy and I sit with a group of Muslim students and faculty at Georgetown University. We are sharing about how in this time of Trumpism we all feel collectively exhausted. We are tired of telling people we encounter every day that we are not terrorists. We are running out of words.

One of the young women in the group tells us that she was recently walking home when a guy — a white guy — approached her threateningly, raised his fist at her hijab, and, his face flushed and angry, said, "Take that rag off your head!"

"I couldn't even respond," the young woman says. "I didn't yell, I didn't cry — I couldn't say anything. I just walked away."

"I know," another young woman wearing a hijab says. "It was too much."

"I'm just so — tired," the first woman says.

"So am I," the second woman says.

172

■ ■ ■ ■

The following week, back home in Dawson.
"Maya!" Musarrat shouts up the stairs.
"You're going to be late!"

Moments later, Maya's sock-clad feet slap
down the stairs. She gets to the bottom,
plants herself on the landing in front of us,
and starts pulling on her boots. She is wearing a head scarf, wound carefully around
her head.

"Let's go," she says, standing, heading
toward the front door.

"Wait," I say. I nod at her. This is the first
time she has ever chosen to wear a head
scarf to school. "Are you sure you want to
wear a head scarf?"

"Yeah. I want to look like Mommy."

She stands straighter, juts her chin. She
oozes with confidence.

"Are you positive?" Musarrat says.

"Yep."

"What if somebody says something or
looks at you funny?" Musarrat says. "Are
you going to be okay with that?"

"This is what I want to wear," Maya says,
her hand reaching for the doorknob. "I'll
always remember this day. The first time I
wore it at school."

"Well, if you want to take it off at any point —" I say.

Maya — eight years old — tilts her head back toward me and opens the front door. "I'm going to wear it the whole day."

And she does. She wears her hijab the entire day, with pride.

Her choice.

Not mine.

"The strange part is, I didn't even know you were Muslim at first," Mandy told me after we first decided to do this lecture. She found out at church. One day, during a Bible study session, Mandy was reading aloud a passage from Leviticus that included the phrase "Welcome the stranger." The discussion turned to refugees and immigration and became heated.

"Your names came up," Mandy says, recalling the event one night over dinner at our house.

"Our names?"

"You and Musarrat."

Musarrat and Maya sit on either side of her at the dining room table.

"What was the context?" I ask.

Mandy wags her head, purses her lips, and raises her voice in an impression of an unnamed congregant. " 'Well, you know, we have *Muslims* in this community.' "

" 'We do?' " Mandy responds in her own voice.

Back in character as the horrified congregant, Mandy lowers her voice to a stage whisper. " 'Well, you know the wife wears a head thing.' "

" 'A hijab?' "

" 'I guess, yeah, I don't know what you call it. It's a scarf on her head. Do you know why she wears that?' "

Mandy, now speaking as herself, says, " 'Why does she wear a hijab?' "

Mandy leans across the table and, in the voice of the congregant, says, " 'Because . . . *he makes her wear it.*' "

"So," I say to the audience, "the misconception about women. You guys all hear about women in Islam. I hear it all the time. I hear it way too much."

A small laugh ripples through the room.

"Here's the question, right?" I pause. "Why does Dr. Virji make his wife wear that head scarf?"

I shake my head, stare at the podium, then raise my head. "That's a real question someone asked, by the way. So, okay, the misconception: *Islam oppresses women and forces them to cover their hair.*"

175

I raise my hand. "How many people believe that? It's okay. I won't judge. Raise your hand if you're brave. Anybody? No? I guess the brave ones have gone. All right. That statement? That Islam forces women to cover their hair?"

I pause, shake my head.

"Absolutely not," I say. "Now, there are certain countries that have a tribally rooted society that claim to be Muslim. But these countries violate the human rights of women and foreigners left, right, and center. I don't blame you for your feelings against them. I understand where the perceptions come from. Let me give it to you straight."

I rake my finger down the page of my outline. "The prophet Muhammad said, 'A man should respect all women in the world, the womb that bore him.' "

I look up from the page and squint into the audience. "Does that sound like a misogynist to you? Are those the words of a misogynist? Now, Muhammad came along during a time when in the pagan societies, women were nothing. If you gave birth to a daughter — and this is true of many cultures at the time — if you had an infant daughter, you buried her alive."

The people sitting in the rows in front of me literally gasp.

"When Muhammad started giving women rights, the pagans said, 'How dare you? We own them. We buy them. We sell them. We trade them. We beat them. How dare you say they are our equals?' "

I allow the audience reaction to build. I hear people whispering to each other in disbelief, in horror. I wait for the noise to subside, for the audience to settle, I clear my throat and say, "Did you know that in Islam — in the seventh century — Muhammad gave women the right to vote, the right to property, and the right to divorce their husbands? In the *seventh* century. When did women get the right to vote in the United States? I'll tell you. In 1920. Thirteen hundred years later, with the Nineteenth Amendment. Now, yes, certain countries oppress women. They treat women as unequals. It's a sickness of the mind. That is radical. You know what that is? Non-Islam."

I remember the first time I met her, the first time I saw her face, which was also the instant I fell in love with her. Musarrat, my wife.

Allentown, Pennsylvania.

The summer between college and medical school.

I drive from Washington, DC, to Allentown, a nearly four-hour trip, monotonous highway most of the way. I go by myself, taking my time. I find driving — the hum of the wheels on the road, the flow of the passing scenery, the steadiness, the mundanity of keeping my car in the lane — a welcome contrast and distraction to the intensity of premed classwork and studying. On this muggy summer day, I'm on my way to visit my mom's family, a houseful of aunts, uncles, cousins, a swarm of relatives, a loving chaos. With my parents and brothers living in Florida, I visit these relatives often for a hit of family and a taste of halal home cooking.

This day, after I arrive at my aunt's house, I inject myself into the typical swirl of activity — people laughing, loud and lively conversation, feeling the warmth of family around me, the feeling of home. Then, at one point, everything freezes into a sort of tableau, at least that's how I imagine it, and I see myself walking upstairs to the second floor for some reason, just as she walks down —

A young woman, wearing a hijab, moving in what seems like slow motion down the stairs.

She smiles, and, man, I practically tip over.

That's all it takes.

Her smile.

Like a flash of light boring into me, blinding me.

*Wow.*

I think that.

I don't say that aloud.

I don't think I do.

Maybe I actually do say that.

In a nanosecond, a blink of an eye, we pass each other on the stairs.

I turn around and forget where I was going. This young woman — this vision — seizes my mind, my heart. Just like that.

I scramble down the stairs, my eyes locked on her across the room, too overcome to speak to her, not sure if I'm even supposed to without an introduction — we're Muslims, we have rules about dating and courting. But I find my aunt, gossiping in the corner with her friends, and I say, in a whisper, urgently, "Who is that?"

My aunt doesn't move, doesn't look at her. She knows exactly who I mean. Does she have a hand in this? I don't know. I'll never know.

"Musarrat," my aunt says. She's a friend of the family. A neighbor. She comes around often.

I don't get all the details. I don't need all the details.

"I have to" — I swallow, feeling unsteady — "talk to her."

"She's a few years younger than you."

"Okay."

"I'm not sure her parents, or your parents —"

"It's okay," I say, my heart racing.

"We're all going to a picnic later," my aunt says.

"Musarrat, too?"

"I'll see to it," my aunt says.

At the picnic, Musarrat ignores me.

I talk to her, try to engage, crack a couple of jokes. The people around her laugh, but she appears to have no interest in me.

*It's a test,* I think. *Yeah. She's testing me, seeing what I'm made of, if I give up easily. She has to like me, right? I'm educated — I'm going to be a doctor — I clean up nice. Come on. I'm not that bad. Right?*

Definitely a test.

I don't back down. I'm careful not to come on too strong, but I don't give up. Eventually we talk a little, small talk. One time she smiles. I think. Another time she actually laughs. I'm sure about that. But mostly she talks to her friends, my aunt's family, and gives me less than the time of day.

*Just motivates me more,* I tell myself. *I am not giving up.*

"Well," I say, as the sun starts to set, "I have to get back to DC. It's a four-hour drive, so, yeah, I better hit the road —"

I stand up from the picnic blanket, hesitating, brushing invisible blades of grass off myself. Trying to bide my time.

"It was nice meeting you, Musarrat," I say.

She says nothing. I don't know if she's even heard me.

*Oh, I am so not giving up. I will get her attention. I will stand here, pretending to flick fake grass off my shirt all night if I have to.*

"So, yeah, I'll just say good-bye to my aunt —"

After a long silent moment, Musarrat turns her head and cranes her neck toward me. She looks at me with what seems like curiosity, as if I'm some kind of rare creature she's noticed just now for the first time. I smile back.

"Do you plan to come to Allentown again?" she says.

"Hm?" I say, trying to seem disinterested.

Then I realize I'd better not be too coy.

"I mean, yes, I will come back again, you know, sometime."

"Well, if you do, I'd be happy to meet you again."

*Score.*

I feel my cheeks burn.

"In that case, I'll come back soon," I say.

She turns away. But before she does, I catch her smile.

I return to Allentown to see my aunt a week or so later, and she makes sure to invite Musarrat. After that, Musarrat and I start talking on the phone regularly. It takes six phone calls for me to know I will marry her. I propose, she accepts, and we begin the process of planning the arrangements.

Musarrat and I both have a lot of family in Toronto, so we decide to get married there. We have a traditional big blowout Indian wedding: five hundred people, tons of food, music, dancing, celebrating, and partying every night for five nights in a row.

I love that tradition — a short engagement followed by a long wedding celebration, symbolizing a long and lasting marriage.

I peer at the page and again read from my notes, "First Corinthians 11:5–7: 'Any woman who prays in public with nothing on her head, she might as well shave her head. Since shaving her head is shameful, she should cover her head.' "

I jolt my head up quickly and say, "This is Paul writing a letter to Corinthians. He is telling women, cover your head. That's why Mennonite Christians cover their hair. That's why Coptic Christians cover their hair. So. Why are Muslims doing this? We could say we're following the Bible."

A few scattered laughs, a shuffling of feet, seats squeaking.

"We *should* say we're following the Bible, because it doesn't say anything like that in the Quran. The Quran says dress modestly. It doesn't say cover this or cover that. That was later, statements from Muhammad."

I then smile, maybe a little mischievously, and I say, "So, let me ask you a question. Have you ever seen a picture of the Virgin Mary — Jesus's mother — without her hair covered?"

I glance at my daughter, sitting in the front row, squirming a little as she catches me looking at her. I direct the question to her, feeling myself smile.

"So, Maya, have you? Think about it."

She giggles, shakes her head, and mouths, "No."

I rest my elbows on the podium, lean into the audience, and say, "Let's all think about it. Answer from your heart. If she were here right now, the Virgin Mary, Jesus's mother — what would she wear? Would she wear a tank top, or would she be dressed?"

I hear a ripple of embarrassed laughter.

"It's interesting. In Christianity, Eve gave the apple to Adam, to man, and she was responsible for man's downfall."

This time I wait for the reaction I know I will hear — a few tense reflexive giggles, a muttering, a few people agreeing aloud, more audience members moving to get comfortable in their chairs — and I say, "That's not the story in the Quran. In the Quran, they ate the apple together. There is no blame on the woman. In the Quran it says it multiple times. Women are your equals. They are your equals."

*Ultima Skincare.*

6th Street, Dawson, Minnesota.

Musarrat Virji, owner, proprietor, aesthetician.

She accepts walk-ins, but due to popular demand, you may have to wait unless you have an appointment.

As long as I have known her, Musarrat, my wife, mother of our children, a Muslim woman who proudly chooses to wear a hijab, has maintained her independence in every sense. She supports me, and I support her. We see ourselves as your average American couple, your average Muslim couple. We know that the people of Dawson

184

have never seen anything like us. What's unusual is that there is really nothing to see. We are that normal.

Musarrat started with skin care when she was twelve years old.

"I taught myself to do hair removal on my own," she says. "Growing up one of three girls, money was always tight. My parents couldn't always afford to take us girls for these services. I just decided I would teach myself threading, our hair removal process of choice."

She went through a lot of trial and error, convincing her cousins to be her first clients. She showed talent from the start and in a short time became good enough at it to believe she could make skin care a career. After we got married, had kids, and moved to Florida, she enrolled in school to train to be an aesthetician.

She went through an accelerated program, got her license and certification, and opened her own business in Clearwater. When we moved to Pennsylvania, she worked for somebody else, but that just didn't feel right. Every decision had to go through a manager. She wanted more freedom. She wanted her own place. A year or so after we moved to Dawson, she started her own salon.

"I wasn't sure what to expect," she says. "I had no idea what people here were doing. They obviously got their hair and nails done, but what about taking care of their skin?" Musarrat wasn't sure if her services would appeal to the women in town, so she started by working part-time, three days a week, closing her spa at three when the kids got out of school.

"I worked this schedule for the first month or two, and then word began to spread. I expanded my hours, then soon I had to go to full-time. I now get people of all ages, from teenagers to women in their seventies. It's been crazy. My clients tell me, 'Everyone is going to come to you, and not just from Dawson.' "

They're right. People have been coming from all over. Musarrat has regular clients who travel from as far away as Sioux Falls and Minneapolis. She's had people from California. All from referrals and word of mouth. She attracts a lot of first-timers, people who have never before set foot in a spa. I often say it's harder to get an appointment with her than with me.

The audience hums. The subject of women, and in particular women's equality according to Islam, has hit some kind of nerve.

"Women are your equals," I say, catching Musarrat's eye, as she smiles at me. Looking back into the audience, I say, "What differentiates you is your righteousness. Now, let me take this one step farther. I feel like I'm speaking for my wife — she would normally speak for herself — but from the Muslim woman's perspective, she actually feels that the Western woman is the one who is oppressed. Can you believe that?"

I absently rub my neck, then drop my hand and gesture toward the rows in front of me. "Do you feel oppressed?"

I hold, waiting for a reaction that I know will not come.

"No," I say. "I know you don't feel oppressed. But what the Muslim woman says — now, think about this — you have beauty contests where women wear thongs and bikinis and are judged by men like they're cattle. You don't think that's diminishing? That is diminishing. We live in a society where a woman's looks get her promoted, where the more you show, the better off you are. Talk to people. That happens. That's real. You don't feel stuck that way? Okay, now, let's neutralize that idea."

I pause for a moment, dropping my head, and say quietly, "You respect me for my mind, not for the rest of me. That is the

Islamic concept. That's what we try to get at. It's modesty. It's the idea that modesty is a paragon."

I gesture toward Musarrat, and I say, "Why is it that she is oppressed because she covers her hair? Is a nun oppressed? Is a Coptic Christian or a Mennonite oppressed? Is a woman who is cold and puts a scarf on . . . is she oppressed? I mean, really, who *cares*?"

I shake my head for two, three, five full seconds, and I whisper, "It's an inner manifestation. It is something you feel inside. Each person — each woman — is an individual. My mom doesn't wear a hijab. I don't care. It's what you feel in *here.*"

I pat my chest and then blink, as a thought has suddenly occurred to me. "It's a symbol, almost like wearing a cross. Right? You are reflecting your behavior through a symbol, something visual. If you *don't* wear a cross, does that mean you're bad?"

I hold, allow the obviousness of this statement to penetrate the auditorium, and say quickly, "No. Of course not. That's ridiculous. It's what's in your heart. That is just another extension of you. That's a symbol. That's your flag. That's good to do that. Let it be known. Let it be with you. That is how we — we Muslims — see it." And then I feel my voice lowering, as I say, "So when you say, 'Dr. Virji forces his wife —' "

I hear myself snicker ironically, and then I retreat and say with insistence, "I didn't force her. She can wear whatever she wants."

I suddenly feel trapped by the podium, enclosed in a tiny invisible box. I want to bust out, prowl the stage. Instead I breathe and press my hands into the sides of the lectern.

"Now, your response to me should be, 'Okay, well, why don't men do it, right?' " I wave my hand above my head. "Anybody? Where are the brave ones? Ask me. Okay. Well, let's talk about that. I mean, it's a good question. Why don't men do it?"

I pause for effect because I can see and hear the audience in front of me, wondering, anticipating, wanting that answer.

"Well," I say, "men in Islam had the first hijab. It is an invisible one. Not one that you put on your hair but an imperative to turn away when you see something that stimulates you lustfully. If you see a woman who is scantily dressed or wearing something provocative, you should turn away — and that's the hijab."

I let this new concept sink in and settle — the thought of it, the metaphor, the meaning so profound to me when I first accepted and adopted it.

"Now, remember, this life is nothing, right? This is an optical illusion. We are interested in the afterlife. But in this life, physical stuff is important. If it wasn't important, you wouldn't have people with their bodies on magazine covers or provocatively dressed in Hollywood, and so forth."

I hear a tiny sound on my left side. An abrupt rustling of paper, a clearing of a throat, some kind of noise, a distraction. I look toward Musarrat and see a look on her face that I know well. She widens her eyes and nods meaningfully. "Move this along," she's thinking. "Ayaz, I love you, but — *wrap it up.*"

I grin, fail to stifle the oncoming laugh, and say, "I'm being reminded to be brief." I shrug, nodding in Musarrat's direction.

The audience laughs.

"All right. Moving along," I say. "Okay, this is Jesus: 'Who wants to possess her is guilty of adultery. So if your right eye causes you to sin, gouge it out and throw it away.' "

*Rough words,* I think. *Graphic.*

"Imagine a relationship where the sex — where the *love* — that exists between a man and a woman is not everywhere," I say. "Imagine that the man lusts for his wife and the wife covers herself because she doesn't

190

want the lust of other men. Imagine that relationship. See, what's happened in modern society is that sex has been externalized. Men are supposed to crave other women. You're supposed to go after sexuality. Traditionally, what's one of the number one magazines sold in this country? I don't know if it is now, but seven years ago or so, it was *Playboy.* Why? Is it because men are looking at the stories, at the articles? What does that husband's wife say about that? Now. Imagine a relationship where the wife knows the husband is out there *not* looking. He is doing his work, and he comes home and his passions are directed toward her. Not to this celebrity or that image. That's the vision of Islam."

I wait, wondering if my words have landed.

"That's why the men are different than the women. We have different bodies. We have a different emotional makeup. Men are very physical. They want to possess. So men have to turn away. If I don't do that, who knows? God. Who pays for it? I do. You can't see my hijab, my head covering, because it's invisible. But it's there. It doesn't matter whether you see it. Somebody else sees it. God sees it."

Suddenly I feel so exhausted, not from speaking but from explaining, from trying to make these four hundred people in front of me *see*. Or at least to make them understand an alternative perspective.

And then I recall a recent incident that makes me smile.

A woman I know slightly is waiting for my friend Doug in the town's grocery store, which he manages. First the cashier and then the stock clerk asks if they can help her.

"No," the woman says, "I'm waiting for Doug."

Finally Doug has a free moment and approaches the woman.

"What can I do for you?" he asks.

"Well, actually, I want to give you a hug."

"Oh." Doug shrugs and starts to move toward her, then stops. "Why?"

"I don't really want to hug you," the woman says. "I'd like to hug Ayaz, but I don't know if I'm allowed to. He's done so much for the community. I just wanted to thank him. I thought I'd hug you and you could pass it on to him because the two of you are friends."

"All right," Doug says.

"Are they allowed to hug?"

"You mean Muslims?"

The woman's cheeks flush. "Yes."

"I hug him all the time." Doug shrugs again. "Tell you what. I'm going to see him tonight. He's not a big hugger, but I'm going to give him two hugs, one from me and one from you, and I'll make sure I tell him which is which, okay?"

"Thank you," the woman says.

And she hugs Doug, my dear friend, my hug-in stand-in.

# 10
## SHARIA LAW

I bend my knees, inhale deeply, exhale slowly, allowing a thin soft whistle of air to escape. The talk has come to its last point.

"Sharia," I say. "Sharia law."

Those two words send the audience into what feels like a grave silence. I can almost sense their dread. The word carries such weight, such foreboding.

"Muslims want to impose Sharia law in the United States and in the West, right?" I say. "Sharia law. You hear it all the time."

I then say the words rhythmically, almost as if I'm chanting a jingle, or singing a children's song —

"Sharia. Sharia law. Sha-ree-ah."

They must think I am profane. Or crazy.

"But," I say, "you don't even know what it means."

I soften my voice, and say, "Sharia means — literally translated — a path to giving water. To life — giving water. That is the definition of Sharia. Jesus said in Matthew 5:17, 'Do not think I have come to do away with the law of Moses and the teachings of the prophets. I have come not to do away with them but to make their teachings come true.' "

I pause, and with a plea lodged in my throat, I say, "Sharia is a construct. For the Muslim, it is an understanding of how to elevate yourself spiritually by following certain rules and regulations. And for those of you who are nervous, don't be. Wait until you hear what those rules and regulations are. They are about goodness, living your life according to *goodness*."

I close my eyes and think about that idea. Goodness.

I think about what it means to me.

Goodness, I believe, means hope. It means helping. It means that I try to live for my patients, all of them, but especially the ones at the bariatric clinic I started here. They are my constants. Many of them came here believing that I was their last hope, their only hope. I am so committed to them. I will help them. I know that I will change their lives. What they don't know is that each one of them is changing mine.

"Sharia law," I repeat in the auditorium, my voice dissolving into a new level of hurt.

I can sense that I don't have much time left in my lecture. I sneak a peek at the remaining pages of my outline, see only two, cough, and prepare to power through to the end.

"Sharia law is broken down into five constructs," I say. "One is called *adab,* which means manners and morality. Example. In Islam, it says you should smile at your neighbor. And if your neighbor does something unkind to you, you have to give them seventy benefits of the doubt. So if you're thinking, 'You know, so and so didn't say hi to me today,' well, maybe he was tired. Or maybe he didn't see me. Maybe he was distracted or worried about something. *Seventy* benefits of the doubt. That's what we owe our neighbor. I mean, I'll be honest, two, three, I can barely get there. Seventy? But that's part of our Sharia construct, before we start backbiting our neighbor or deciding 'Hey, that guy is evil' or whatever, we need to give the benefit of the doubt. We need to show our good manners. That is *adab.* Love thy neighbor. That's what it's about."

I go on. "Another construct. *Ibadah.* Ritual practices. In Islam, one of our ritual practices is charity. We have to give 2.5 percent of our possessions — of our income

— to charity. So. Is that a bad thing? Is that something I shouldn't impose on myself? I don't think so. I think it's a good thing. We are instructed to be charitable. That, too, is Sharia."

The audience rustles, getting comfortable not just in their seats but *with the constructs,* I think, and I nod and continue, "Here is another construct. *I'tiqada.* Belief in one God. We believe that there is one God and whatever you do, you will be in front of Him again. So don't think that this world ends when you die. No. That's when it *begins. You* begin, and you will account for all of it, for everything you've done."

I pause for a beat and a transition, and I say, "Construct number four, *Mu'mamalat,* which are transactions and contracts, such as marriage. And then, last, *'Uqubat,* which is punishments for crimes. Those are the five constructs."

I look into the audience, conscious of my internal clock ticking, knowing that I am coming to the end of the lecture.

"Muhammad never imposed Sharia on others. He imposed it on Muslims. There were non-Muslims — Jews, Christians, atheists, pagans, agnostics — who lived peacefully in his society. That's the way it goes. Only that way. You can work. You can live.

197

You can do whatever you like. You may not impose."

I lower my voice into a whisper again, and say, "Here is a perfect example. I'm a Muslim. I believe in Muhammad's prophethood. I believe there is one God. I believe in the Quran. According to my religion, I may not drink alcohol. So I don't. I impose that on myself. That is Sharia. Now . . ."

I point into the audience, thrusting my finger with an intensity I don't expect and don't intend. "I may not impose that on anybody else. If you — if you and I, if any of us — were to go to Dubai and we were to sit in a restaurant, and you and I were to order wine, a glass of wine, the waiter will ask me, 'Are you Muslim?' I will say, 'Yes.' And he will say, 'I can't give it to you. It's forbidden.' "

I glance into the audience, and I see people with their mouths open. Their eyes are fixed on me, their expressions stunned, frozen on their faces.

"I would be breaking the law," I say. "Now, if you were a Christian and not a Muslim and you said, 'I would like a glass of wine,' the waiter would still ask you, 'Are you a Muslim?' You would say, 'No.' The waiter would say, 'Fine. What kind of wine do you want? Here is the wine list, the beer, our other alcohol, whatever.' You can have what you want. No problem. You eat pork? No problem. It is not forbidden to you.

"That is Sharia. Not what some other . . . *people* . . . are saying. Forget about that. If you have other information, challenge me. If you know something else about Sharia that I don't know, show me, please."

It's ridiculous, I know, absurd, but I feel both unsteady and thrilled at the same time.

"Sharia," I say again, in a hush. "Sharia to us is a stepping stone to *Tariqa. Tariqa* is the oneness of God, the knowledge, the understanding. I guess you could equate it to Nirvana for Buddhism. So that to us —"

I feel my forehead furrowing and my hands opening and closing as I attempt to explain this idea — this feeling — that is so difficult to grasp. This is a slippery idea that has eluded me my entire life.

"Sharia is this — nothing," I say. "To do it without the heart means nothing. It's —"

I smile as an example occurs to me. I have drifted far from my notes even as I know I have nearly come to the end of my lecture, except for the handful of wrap-up slides I will project on the screen behind me.

"It's the difference between prohibition and not drinking alcohol," I say, grinning, this analogy striking a chord. "Prohibition is a law that stops you from doing it. You actually think it's okay to drink alcohol, but you don't do it because of the law. Whereas I abstain because I think it's right. I believe it's the right thing to do. That's the difference. That's Sharia. You do it for *yourself.*"

I wave my hand above my head. I feel as if I am reaching toward the heavens. "These are the ways to elevate yourself so that you may know Him. That is the Islamic paragon. Sharia is a guide. It is spiritual health and physical health."

My voice races, my pulse pounds. "We have bodies, too. So there are laws of cleanliness. You have to be clean. You shouldn't make a mess."

I hear her then. Her rustling, murmuring, throat clearing — I can't decipher the exact sound but I hear it, like the final bell ringing to end the school day.

I lean my body away from the podium and see Pastor Mandy gesturing in the shadows in front of me.

*I need to finish,* I think. No, I *am* finished.

I glance at my notes and see that I still have those two pages left to go, but I slide back behind the podium and I say more to Mandy than to the audience, "Okay. Again, the brevity. So, we will just —"

I riffle through my notes, find the final

quote I want to share. "Here, in Proverbs, 31:4–7, Solomon is saying, 'Kings should not drink wine nor have a craving for alcohol. When they drink, they forget the laws and ignore the rights of people in need. Alcohol is for people who are dying and for those in misery.' "

I look up and hear my voice trail off. "Okay, so is it again that we Muslims are following the Bible? A question for you."

I'm rambling. I'm trying to find a proper ending, the appropriate wrap-up, but I can't. I shake my head and sigh. I have no neat verbal ribbon with which to tie up my lecture.

So I just stop.

"All right," I say. "I'm just not going to go anymore. We'll go to the slides now. So I'm going to end because I'm forced to. I'm just kidding."

The audience laughs with me.

*I have them,* I realize. *They're with me.*

And this, I also realize, is a mild surprise.

"Okay," I say, twisting toward the screen behind me. "I'm going to show you some final pictures. Can we put that up?"

"Yes."

It's Pastor Mandy speaking from the shadows, from the ether, and then I glance back and forth between the large screen and the audience.

"Some final reflections," I say, "to show you how Islamophobia, this Muslim ban, this 'All Muslims are terrorists,' this wall affects regular people, folks I know. These are real."

Click.

A photo of a fax — all in caps — appears on the screen behind me.

I stare at it, and even though I have seen it a dozen times, the dark, cold rage I felt when I first read it still grips my chest.

I speak to the audience over my shoulder as I say, "This is a fax my brother, who is an investment adviser in Orlando, got right after the election."

Then, my voice quavering, not from the laryngitis, but from anger spewing into my throat, I read, "GET THE *F* OUT OF MY COUNTRY. YOU MUSLIM PIG!"

"Yeah, my brother got this," I say, riveted on the screen behind me, and I begin reading the fax again, but this time I'm only able to make it six words in: "Get the *F* out of my country . . ."

I turn to the audience, and I say, my voice lilting high with incomprehension, "And the lady was bold enough to put her *name* — Susan — and her company in Chicago. She's *welcoming*. She's like, 'You can't even do anything about it because Donald Trump is in town. *I'm* allowed to do this.' I mean, can you imagine the audacity? This is *real*. This is happening."

I want to scream. The sense memory of the wave of anger that hit me — that flattened me on the day of the election — now curdles inside me.

"The next slide," I say, feeling a sudden impulse to grit my teeth but talking softly. "This happened to a friend of ours in Florida. She went to her car in her driveway, and, okay, I'll read this, 'Trump gonna deport ur *terrist* sand n-word. Get you're A.S.S. back out of my U.S.A. Christ not Allah.' "

I face the audience, my arms spread wide in helplessness, in disbelief, in horror.

"Is that what Jesus would do?"

"No," a few people in the audience say timidly.

I guess I'm secretly hoping that the audience would have responded with more force, with an equally horrified *NO*, because I repeat the question, "Is that would *Jesus* would do?"

"No!" the audience says, louder, indignantly.

"Now, this could be me," I say. "This could be me tomorrow."

I drop my head and say to the audience, again speaking hurriedly, almost breathlessly, "To finish this story. These people, who are friends of my brother, later on, a week or so later, went to the graveyard to visit their late mother and they found Trump-Pence stickers all over the tombstones."

*I want to hear their outrage,* I think, peering into the stone-faced audience. *I have shown them these stories, this hatred, where is their outrage?*

"Is this Jesus?" I say. "Should I take that — should I accept that — and say, 'This is Jesus. This is what Christians are like?' No. You know I won't do that. I would never do that. But I want you to understand the paradigm. I want you to understand the double standard."

I sigh, and then I say, quietly, my words suddenly engulfed by sadness, "I just want you to understand. I want you to understand where I'm coming from. I want you to know why I'm here."

My back to the audience, I gesture at the screen and say, "Next slide."

Behind me the cover of a magazine appears. Six young people wearing lab coats stand beneath a two-line tower of orange letters proclaiming the title of the magazine,

*Modern Healthcare.* Below the young people, the following two-sentence paragraph screams, "American healthcare relies on immigrants. Industry leaders and medical researchers want President Trump to know it."

I face the audience, give them a moment to read the slide, and then hitch my thumb over my shoulder.

"You think this doesn't affect you?"

I take a beat.

"Think twice," I say.

I wait for the murmuring in the audience to quiet.

"Okay, you might say, 'Well, who cares, there's a bunch of refugees out there, fine. You can make that argument.' You might say, 'Well, who cares about justice for brown people?' like me."

Pin-drop quiet.

"Sure. No problem."

I lean forward, my body coiled over the top of the podium, and, my voice rasping, ask, "But what about you? Does this affect you? This Muslim ban?"

I thumb at the screen behind me, at the six young people in lab coats.

"These are scientists from Harvard."

A hum pulsates through the audience, and I can feel it — a mess of emotions . . .

discomfort, shock, outrage . . . I can't identify them all.

"These scientists," I say, "are Iranian scientists who can't get into this country. America used to attract the greatest minds in the world. That's why we are amazing."

Now the audience grumbles. I'm thrown for a moment until I realize they are grumbling in *agreement*. I feed off this. "You know why we are amazing? Because Solomon said in Proverbs 1:22, 'Foolish people, how long do you want to be foolish? How long will you enjoy making fun of knowledge and education and enlightenment?' "

I make a fist and punch toward the audience. "We are kicking smart people *out*," I say. "The National Rural Health Association has put out a big article. We have a problem with doctors in rural America. They're not coming here. And you know who fills those voids?"

I pause for what feels like ten seconds, and I say, slapping my chest to indicate myself, "Immigrant doctors."

My throat feels hot and rough, and I hear my voice rise as I say, "We have a problem now. So you should think, 'Oh, well, but, yeah, it's not affecting me. It's not affecting me in Dawson because I've got our doctors here. They're here.' "

I nod, lean into the microphone and say, "Think again. On Saturday, I'm going to Dubai. My mother is sick. She was having chest pains. She was in Kenya. They flew her over there. I am going to see my mother. Now."

I take a step back and lower my voice.

"I have a stamp on my passport for Iraq because I went there last year for a spiritual pilgrimage. We Muslims believe Noah is buried in Iraq in Najaf, as well as Adam, so I went there to pay my respects to them as my prophets. When I come back on a Thursday, I have patients on Friday. If the authorities detain me — which I'd say is a fifty-fifty chance — any of you who are seeing me on Friday, well, I don't know if you will. It's fifty-fifty. Now it's affecting *you*."

I pause.

"This is real," I say in a whisper. "Just last week, a Muslim physicist — *born in this country,* a US citizen, went to Chile. He worked for NASA. He went to Chile to race solar cars because that's his hobby. They wouldn't let him back into the country. They went through his iPhone, and they said, 'You have to give us your password.' He said, 'I can't. I work for NASA. This is confidential information.' Because he's *Muslim.* Really?"

Now I hear it.

Clearly.

The audience has turned.

They share my outrage.

Not all of them, I'm sure. Not the whole four hundred. But the energy of outrage crackles through the crowd like an electrical shock.

*We're in this together,* I think. *For this one moment, we share this.*

I could be in my living room, talking to friends.

I could be in Dubai, relating this story.

I could be in a mosque, praying.

But I'm here in Dawson.

And I feel — full.

I speak quickly now, gesturing toward the audience. "And remember that Muslim fencer that won all those medals in Rio?"

The audience reacts in agreement.

I don't know if they actually do remember her, but they feel empathy for her already, for the hardship they are anticipating that I am about to share.

"Guess what happened to her when she tried to come into the country? She wears a hijab like my wife. Guess what happened to her? Think."

They know. I don't have to tell them. They *know.* I just nod.

I press on.

"We know a family," I say. "She is a Muslim immigration attorney. This is real. She is a United States citizen. She's married to a Canadian citizen. One night they crossed the border in Michigan to have dinner with their in-laws in Canada."

I pause and finish with pain staining my voice.

"They couldn't come back."

I feel my voice lift as I say, "Now, what happens if I can't come back? Who is going to see you? Dr. Grong is already busy."

A roar of laughter.

I wait for the crowd to quiet, and then I say, "So if you think it doesn't affect you, think again."

I whip around to the screen behind me.

"Next slide."

A photo flashes, showing a plaque of the seal of the United States Supreme Court with the inscription below it: "Prophet Muhammad honored by U.S. Supreme Court as one of the greatest lawgivers of the world in 1935."

I point at the slide, gesturing at it, flailing at it.

"I've cited this before, and people were shocked. You don't believe me?"

I hear the audience murmuring as they

209

read the inscription.

"Go look at the Supreme Court," I say. "It honors Muhammad, *my* Muhammad, as one of the greatest lawgivers of all time. Okay?"

I can't turn away from it. I point at the Supreme Court seal and the words "Prophet Muhammad," and I actually feel overcome with emotion, with pride, and I say, my voice lowering, "I put this up because I wanted people to see it. Even if you don't believe me, go look at it. It's there, okay. It is."

I face the audience, swallow, and ask, "Are there any other slides? I think so. Can you go to the next slide?"

Click.

A photograph of me, Faisal, and Maya standing in the hallway outside this auditorium appears.

The audience laughs in recognition.

"Oh, yeah," I say, looking up at the slide. "So, real brown people."

A bigger laugh.

"We're *normal.* We're at the theater. Maya, Faisal, and myself. Next one, please."

The audience continues laughing as a photo of our two cats lying on our bed, snuggling against each other, clicks on.

"That's our cats. They're not terrorist cats."

A massive laugh. It comes with such force that I grip the podium for support. I have to pause before I can continue.

"Last slide," I say, facing the screen.

Click.

Twenty people, children, two women wearing hijabs, a couple of men, including me, all of us smiling, stand in front of a doorway to a house.

"More brown people," I say.

I turn back to the audience.

"That's my family in Dubai. Guess what we're doing? We're having fun. We're going to a theme park. We're going four-wheeling in the desert. Maya held a falcon for the first time in her life. That's what we do. Normal stuff. We're normal. I have problems like any of you. I've got an adolescent who doesn't listen to me."

A thunderclap of laughter, by far the biggest of the night. A laugh that hits like a wave, knocking me back on my heels. A stand-up comic's dream.

I grin widely, shake my head, and say, "I've got the same things you have, okay? So. Understand this. This is the ninety-nine percent. That's who we are. Now Musarrat and Maya want to say a few words, but I will conclude with this. It has been an honor to talk to you."

I bow slightly, reflexively, and step away from the podium. As I do, I hear a sound, something unfamiliar and unexpected. The audience is roaring, and then, almost as one, as if it was choreographed, they rise. They stand, applauding, shouting, whistling.

I'm beyond thrown. I'm humbled, and I am deeply moved. The crowd keeps applauding, clapping — for how long, I can't say — and then finally Musarrat and Maya climb up onto the stage and come toward me, both of them looking as happy and as thrown as I feel. Maya says something to Musarrat, who leans down to hear her. And then Musarrat releases Maya's hand, and my daughter, who has turned nine years old today, walks with confidence and purpose to my side. She looks up at me expectantly. She wants to say something to the audience. I have no idea what. This is unrehearsed, spontaneous.

I lower the microphone to her, and with the instinct of a polished, experienced performer or public speaker, she waits for the audience's reaction to peak and then subside.

I look at her and hesitate, debating whether to announce that today is her birthday. But before I can, I hear Doug shout out, "Happy birthday, Maya!"

The crowd claps, several people shout "Happy birthday!," and then Maya, momentarily gone shy, retreats. She quickly composes herself, giggles, and anchors her slight frame next to the podium. Then, facing the four hundred people in front of her, with deep conviction and a natural confidence I could never have summoned at her age, she summarizes my lecture — indeed, my mission — in three simple words, the most powerful words of the night.

She grips the microphone tight and whispers, "God bless everyone."

# 11
## BREATHE

Nearly two years and twenty lectures later, Maya's message — those three words — more than resonate with me. They describe my purpose, inform my belief, refuel my passion to go on. I hear my daughter's words when I have felt the urge to quit.

More than once I have thought of leaving the country. During the president's blatant racism and anti-Semitism when groups of neo-Nazis gathered and marched in Charlottesville ("Some very good people on both sides") — and so many other horrifying moments — watching him cozy up to the North Korean dictator and seeing children, some of them infants, ripped out of their parents' arms at the US border, and placed in cages. At too many times, I don't recognize my country. But I've decided to go on because the lectures have become more than just a practicing Muslim trying to dispel the myths about his religion. They've become an act of love. And this action has been hard.

*Doing the right thing, doing something that matters, even to a few, is hard,* I remind myself. *It's supposed to be hard.*

And then I hear my daughter's voice and I ask myself —

*If not me, then who?*

In contrast to the protests and angry phone calls that came into the school before my lecture in Dawson, afterward I receive an outpouring of support. When I wake up the next morning, I open my email inbox and see dozens of letters of thanks, some expressing love. By the next month, that number swells to more than seven hundred.

The week after my lecture, patients acknowledge how much they learned. People stop me on the street and come over to me in Wanda's Diner to thank me. Then Pastor Mandy tells me that I have been invited to give my "Love Thy Neighbor" lecture in Montevideo, a neighboring town three times the size of Dawson. Still feeling high from the overwhelming positive response to my lecture, I accept.

"You're spreading the word," Pastor Mandy says.

A month later, Pastor Mandy, Musarrat,

Maya, and I pile into Doug's van and head to the Montevideo Public Library, twenty minutes away. When we pull up in front of the library, I find seventy-five people waiting for me, several of them brandishing Bibles. As I get out of the van, several men scream Bible verses at me. Doug becomes my bodyguard — a role he will reprise at other events — escorting Mandy, my family, and me into the library.

Once I start my lecture, the large crowd quiets down. My voice has returned to normal, but I deliver my talk haltingly, thrown by the tension I feel in the room.

Since I ran over my allotted time in Dawson and never got to do a formal Q and A, I promised myself and Mandy that I would end my lecture early and allow ample time for questions. Here in Montevideo, the questions come fast and furious, and then someone takes issue with my belief that faith without deeds is meaningless. He says that prayer is all that matters, and then he — or someone else — raises his voice and calls me the anti-Christ. It gets contentious.

I don't back down. In fact, I want to talk to this guy — logically.

"Prayer is all that matters," I say. "Let's take your logic to the next level. So. Nothing I do matters. I'm spending my whole life doing things that don't matter. The free clinics I've worked in for twenty years don't matter. The free clinics I started don't matter. The reason I came to Dawson was to answer the call of rural medicine. I see it as a calling. People need it here — need me here — and I want to give. I want to be part of the life here. If not me, then who?"

No one answers the rhetorical question. But I hear the undercurrent of discomfort, the bubbling under of rage. I don't care. I keep going.

"You say that nothing I do matters. Prayer is all that matters. You believe I have nothing in common with you. I am anti-Christian. Okay, fine, if that's what you believe, let's take your logic further. Let's take Gandhi, who was one of the most peaceful persons who ever lived. He said, 'I am no religion, but I am all religions.' According to your logic, he's burning in Hell right now because he's not Christian. He doesn't believe what you believe. But Hitler is in Heaven, living it up with God, because he was trying to purify the Aryan race for the glory of Jesus. On the belt buckle of the Nazis it said, 'God is with us.' So Hitler's in Heaven. By your logic, you have more in common with Hitler than you have with me!"

I don't hear the man's exact verbal response, but I hear a protest of rage and the rumble of the crowd behind him. I should back away, I should stop, but I'm too fired up.

"What are you insulted about?" I say, not in anger but intending to ask an honest question. "You just said that deeds don't matter, and I said you contradicted your own Bible. It says in James 2:26, 'Faith without deeds is nothing.' When the pagan man came to Jesus and said, 'How do I get to heaven, good rabbi?' Jesus says, 'Why does thou call me good? There is only One who is good. It's not me.' And the man says, 'But I want to know, how do I get there?' Jesus says, 'Follow the commandments. Obey the laws. Do not commit adultery. Do not lie. Do not sin. Do not cheat. Do not kill. Love thy neighbor. Worship the Lord thy God.' That's it. Simple. He didn't say, 'Worship me.' He said follow the law. He said, 'I didn't come here to replace the law, I came to complete it.' "

The man doesn't want to hear it. He doesn't want to be convinced. He believes that his faith is the only faith, and he wants me to know that my religion and my Bible, the Quran, is an evil book. Nothing will ever change his mind, certainly not the Muslim doctor from the next town.

*But I'm not here for him,* I think.

I'm here for the 30 percent or so who don't know about Islam but want to learn. They may be scared and they may wonder what they should do because they are so afraid, but they are at least open enough to hear me.

These are the people I'm here for tonight.

I just don't know if I have the strength to do this again.

The crowd has turned. They seem to be backing up the guy who called me the anti-Christ. It's clear that I have lost them. The Bible thumpers outshout everyone else, screaming more verses. Musarrat quickly hustles Maya from the front row to the back of the room, near the exit. Doug stations himself in the middle of us all, watching, on alert. I close down the question-and-answer period, and, unnerved, we leave.

On the way back to Dawson, I tell Pastor Mandy that I've given my last lecture. "I'm not doing this anymore," I say. "I'm done. I never wanted to do this in the first place."

Except that in my heart, I don't feel like quitting. I feel as if I haven't quite finished. And I certainly don't want to be silenced in my own country. *This is my country, too,* I think. I have something to say, and I should be given the opportunity to say it. Then I do a sort of internal 180. I will not be shouted down. I don't think we're done yet.

I hear of two editorials that appear in the local Montevideo newspaper. The first, printed a day or so before my talk, comes with the headline "Islam: Not a Religion of Peace." In the editorial, the writer posits a series of falsehoods that she has taken from a virulent anti-Muslim website. I respond with an editorial of my own, the counterpoint to this one, which I title "Islam: A Religion of Peace."

I dispute her point by point, providing links from legitimate sources that back up everything I say. I conclude my editorial by saying, "As a Muslim American, I believe the strength of our Constitution and the American values we struggle for including justice, liberty, equality, and the rule of law are what make America great. I hope we do not fall into the traps that ISIS and divisive politics have set for us. We should not stereotype or condemn our fellow citizens based on religion. Jesus reminds us in Matthew 12:25, 'Any country that divides itself into groups which fight each other will not last very long. And any town or family that divides itself into groups which fight each other will fall apart.' "

After my editorial appears, the Montevideo newspaper prints another editorial that apologizes for the hostile response I received from some of the attendees at my talk. "This is not who we are," the editorial essentially says. It is backing me up.

*No,* I think. *I am not done.*

Pastor Mandy calls me with more invitations to speak, including one in Granite Falls, another neighboring town that went overwhelmingly for Trump. I'm motivated now. I want to do it.

"That's a tough town," Doug says. "I'm going with you, and I'll be packing."

"You what?"

"I will be carrying a weapon. A firearm. I'm licensed."

"Do you really think someone's going to *shoot* me?" I say.

"Not during the lecture," Doug says.

"That's a relief."

"But maybe on your way to the car."

A few hours before the Granite Falls lecture, a neighbor, someone who works in security, comes to my house with a bulletproof vest. I'm dubious, but Doug's description of the town has put me on edge. With my neighbor's help, I wriggle into the bulletproof vest and adjust it to my chest. I find it incredibly uncomfortable and confining.

"I'm not going to wear this," I say, shrugging out of it. "I'll take my chances."

Escorted by my bodyguard, Doug, I give my lecture at the Granite Falls City Hall. The town may have gone heavily for Trump, but in contrast to my reception in Montevideo, the people in attendance here are open and welcoming and I receive an enthusiastic response after I end my talk. During the question-and-answer period, a woman says, "I just want to thank you. These conversations are very much needed."

I call on a man who seems nervous. He starts talking and says, "I want to say, I hear a lot of pain from you."

A hush falls over the crowd.

The man hesitates and then says, "Um . . . I'm sorry."

A reporter from the *Washington Post* attends the Granite Falls lecture and publishes an excellent article about it. I'm deluged with another wave of emails and letters, the vast majority of them positive and some surprising. Hillary Clinton writes me a warm letter of thanks, and Senator Al Franken calls to offer his support. Almost immediately, Pastor Mandy schedules more lectures. I speak at a mosque, and in the fall

Mandy and I are invited to go to Washington, DC, to participate in an interfaith conference at Georgetown Medical School and to speak at George Washington University. I feel that I am starting to be heard — that maybe, just maybe, these talks are making a small difference.

But then one night at dinner at our house, Mandy shares a disturbing story.

"For eleven years in a row, the intern at Grace Lutheran has been asked to do the Memorial Day service in Veterans Park. It's a huge honor. You get to lead the prayers. You do the entire service. It ends with a twenty-one-gun salute."

"It's a very big deal," Doug confirms from across the table.

"So," Mandy says, drawing the word out. "I am the first intern not to be asked."

We all go silent at the table.

"Because of your association with us," Musarrat says.

"You're a Muslim lover," I say.

"What was their reasoning?" Jason asks. "What did they say?"

"Pastor Kendall said there was a rumor that I am quote *not patriotic* unquote."

"They mean you don't love Jesus," I say.

"Well, and then I heard, I should say, somebody *told* me they don't like what I

223

did with you."

"Our talks," I say. "Love thy Muslim."

"I really wanted to do this," Mandy says. "I got so excited. I was like, oh my gosh, I'll be leading this service and there's going to be guns shooting behind me. Who wouldn't love that?"

"Maybe they changed their policy," Jason says.

"I'm sure," Mandy says.

"We just have to wait a year to see if they ask next year's intern," Jason says.

"I don't bet, but if I did, I'd bet that next year we'll have the intern," I say.

"I'll bet," Jason says.

"Me, too," Doug says.

"Heathens," I say.

And then something worse happens.

One night, after giving a sermon at a church in another town, Mandy approaches her car and finds that someone has smeared bacon across the windshield.

Mandy draws herself up, stands at attention, and then loses it.

When she tells me, I freak out.

I stomp, I pace, I shout.

For two days, I am blind with rage. I can't speak to anyone at work. My staff, Jordan my nurse, and the other nurses avoid me as much as they can. Even Stacey keeps her distance.

Mandy, the actual victim of the act of hatred, has to calm *me.*

"It's like they're stealing something sacred from you," I say to her on the phone when she calls to talk me down.

"I kept saying to myself, 'But I'm a Christian, I am a *Christian.'* It's like they are questioning my belief."

"I am so angry this happened to you," I say.

"We have to continue the lectures," she says. When I don't reply, she repeats, "Ayaz, we have to continue the lectures."

"I know," I say. "I know."

In early fall, outraged by Donald Trump's condemnation of NFL players who kneeled during the national anthem to protest police brutality against black people, I write an impassioned letter to the editor of the *Dawson Sentinel,* our weekly newspaper. Too many people I talk to in town condemn the NFL players, saying they're shaming our military. In my letter, I ask our residents to think for themselves and to seek information on their own. I write about how, after some people accused me of being unpatriotic in my talks, a colonel in the US military wrote me a letter of encouragement, saying I was "doing more for protecting the US Constitution than [he] did in 20 years of service." Patriotism, like faith, is what you do.

I conclude the editorial by quoting Martin Luther King, Jr.: " 'I am certain we need to pray for God's help . . . but we are greatly misled if we think the struggle will be won by prayer. God who gave us minds for thinking and bodies for working, would defeat his own purpose if he permitted us to obtain through prayer what may come through work and intelligence. Prayer is a marvelous and necessary supplement of our feeble efforts, but it is a dangerous substitute . . .' "

I sign my name and wait for the after-shock.

Later that week, I sit across from Musarrat in a booth at Wanda's Diner. I'm jammed at work, but I've managed to sneak away for thirty minutes to grab lunch with my wife. I sip my coffee and devour a pancake the size of a hubcap as Musarrat and I swap stories about our morning, the kids, life. Above the normal hum of conversation, I hear a sudden scraping of chairs, the rustle and swish of movement and approaching footsteps, and then a shadow looms over us. Julia, a

Dawson resident I know casually, a staunch Trump supporter, stands by our booth.

"I want to talk to you about your editorial," she says to me, and then slides into our booth next to Musarrat. The vinyl creaks and hisses as Julia settles in across from me. To give her room, Musarrat edges to the far corner, her eyes wide in astonishment at the intrusion.

"Hi, Julia," I say. "Won't you sit down?"

"I don't agree with what you wrote," she says, jutting her chin forward.

"Okay . . ." I say.

"At all," Julia says.

"That's fine. It's a free country. Was there anything specific that you —"

"We need to pray. We should pray for everybody. We should pray for our president. That's all what we need to do. Nothing else. Just *pray.*"

Julia shoots Musarrat a narrow smile, then leans over to me, her chin practically scraping mine.

"We Christians actually believe that our prayers make it to God," she says.

"Julia, everybody who prays believes that. In any religion. We believe that God hears us. But that's not the point."

"Oh? What is the point?"

"The point is that we should pray, sure,

but we also need to act. That's what Martin
Luther King, Jr., said. I quoted him in my
editorial. Prayer is not a substitute for
deeds. *We are greatly misled if we think the
struggle will be won by prayer.* In other
words, you need to act."

"No, you don't." Julia launches herself
backward into the booth and folds her arms.
"I don't care what anybody says. You just
need to pray. That's what Jesus says."

I bite my lip and look down. I tap my
spoon softly against my coffee mug . . .
*ting . . . ting . . . ting . . .* and then I raise my
head and stare at Julia. I find myself fighting the urge to shout.

"So . . . I have it all wrong," I say quietly.

Julia's forehead creases and pulses red.

"You think that because you have Jesus,
your way — your path — is the only one.
You think I'm going to Hell because of what
I believe. Am I right?"

She shifts in her seat. The vinyl sings. Her
eyes flit around the restaurant as if she's
searching for an escape route. She says
nothing, but we both know that is exactly
what she believes.

"So that's it?" I say. "Just pray. That's all
you need to do."

"Yes," Julia says, a murmur.

I don't look up, but I can feel a quiet

descend. I glance at Musarrat. Her mouth has literally dropped open.

"Let me ask you this," I say to Julia. "Do you believe all Muslims should be put on a registry?"

"Absolutely," Julia says. "Of course I do."

"Well," I say, nudging my coffee cup to the side, "look at the time. I have to get back to work. Thanks for the chat, Julia. It was really . . . illuminating."

That night.

The text message pings and blares blue — *Ron is crashing.*

My patient, Ron, ninety-two, who is fighting both terminal heart disease and lung cancer, has begun drowning in his own lung fluid. He can't breathe. I sit at the desk in the nurses' station waiting for Ron to be moved into the OR. I've studied his ultrasound and tested the equipment. As soon as the nurse settles him in, I will perform an emergency pleurocentesis. I'll stick a needle into his chest and drain out as much fluid as I can. This will bring Ron some comfort. This will allow him to breathe.

My phone pings with another text message.

Pastor Mandy.

*Read this,* her text says. I scroll through

comments she's received about my upcoming presentation at Southwestern Minnesota State University.

Nasty comments. Ignorant. Bigoted. Hateful.

I'm shocked. At SMSU, a college campus, I thought I would be speaking to a somewhat liberal audience, or at least to people who would be open-minded. Instead it feels as though I'm walking into an attack.

I place my phone on the desk in front of me and massage the bridge of my nose.

I picture Julia. I think about her self-righteousness, her refusal to acknowledge that there may be another way, that my religion could possibly be as legitimate as hers. She would put all Muslims on a registry — absolutely. She said that to my face. How many more people in Dawson feel that way?

*The number would astonish me,* I think.

I suddenly feel hollowed out, empty. My stomach flips.

I pick up my phone and again scroll through the text Pastor Mandy sent me. "Why am I even doing this?" I ask myself aloud.

I shake my head.

*There are people who don't want me here because I'm a Muslim.*

230

*But everybody wants me here because I'm a doctor.*

Logicians call that a conundrum.

I feel whipsawed, as if I'm riding up and down in the world's most extreme roller coaster.

And then I think about Ron. I picture the procedure. I see myself inserting the needle into his chest, draining out the fluid that's drowning him.

*He has it a lot harder than I do,* I think. *He's fighting for his life.*

But to some extent — aren't I fighting for mine?

My phone pings with a text. It's time.

I walk out of the nurses' station and head toward the ER. I reach the door, and I freeze.

Julia's face floats in front of my eyes. Her chin juts toward me defiantly, her eyes glisten, steely, cold, certain. The simplicity of what she believes rocks me. She's right. I'm wrong. Jesus says so.

Her words ring in my head —

*You just need to pray. That's all we need to do. Just pray.*

"What if I don't go into the ER?" I say aloud. "What if I just stand outside here and pray? What if I did that, Julia? I'm just going to pray that the fluid in Ron's lungs

231

disappears and he starts breathing again. Okay. That should do it. I prayed about it, Julia — I prayed the fluid away."

My hands start to tremble.

"Shake it off," I say to myself. "Come on. Shake it off."

I do. I will Julia's face to dissolve. I compartmentalize. I stay in the moment and put all of my attention on Ron. I conjure his face. That's all I see now. All I see.

I whisper, "Breathe."

I inhale. Then I close my eyes, count to three, and slowly exhale.

With my mind clear, completely centered, I enter the ER and perform the procedure.

I remove a liter and a half of fluid from Ron's lungs. He will make it through the night.

That night I come to a decision. I will continue to give my lectures. I will continue to inform people about my religion. I will keep combating the myths and misinformation about terrorism and Sharia law and how Muslims treat women. I will speak from my heart, with love, passion, dignity, and understanding. I will try to reach as many people as I can, even if that means one person per lecture. SMSU has invited me to speak, and I will. I'll speak because I have to. *If not me, then who?* If I face bigots, deniers, or fools, then I will. Some people face much worse.

I check on Ron the following morning. He's doing beautifully, resting comfortably.

He can breathe.

# 12
## WHAT WILL IT TAKE?

In the month of November 2017 alone, I give five lectures. The flood of emotion after each event wears on me, drains me. At the same time, I reach out to Muslim friends across the country to get a sense of what they're going through. When they relay incidents of bigotry and hatred they've both witnessed and experienced, I feel a new wave of anger, frustration, and helplessness. One night, I speak to an old friend of my brother's who was a year ahead of me in college, an easygoing, extremely likable, hilarious guy, now a successful dentist. Since the election, he's been inundated by vicious comments on Facebook attacking him because he's Muslim, some of the posts written by his own patients.

"I never would have expected this in my own country," he says, sighing, sounding defeated.

This man is a hardworking professional, a

law-abiding citizen, a cancer survivor, and a conscientious contributor to society. He lives in the suburbs and faces the same problems we all do: making a living, paying his bills, raising his kids. He is a typical American.

I live on edge, anticipating the next malicious, venal, incomprehensible, misspelled tweet from our president.

The commander in tweet, I call him.

I wake up each day fearing what I'll read on my phone.

I want to focus on the positive. I sincerely believe that the vast majority of people in Dawson are good, decent people. We simply have a disinformation problem. As a rule, people here watch Fox News regularly. As a result, they are misinformed, and when they talk to each other, they are speaking in an echo chamber. If you are fed only garbage, you not only get used to it, you develop a taste for it. Soon you won't be able to tell when you are actually fed something good, something right, something true.

I look back over the past few months and I think, *I'm tired.*

A year ago, I felt highly motivated to dispel the myths about my faith. I expected to do the one lecture in Dawson. But that first one led to a second and a third and a dozen and local news coverage and national news coverage, the *Washington Post,* NPR, *National Geographic,* and —

I am tired.

I'm tired because my talks, the reactions to my talks — seeing how people really feel, seeing who people really are — have taken me to emotional depths I never imagined. I now see in the world something that goes beyond xenophobia. I see inclusion versus exclusion. I see virtue versus evil. I see love versus hate. I think about the Jordan Peele film *Get Out,* a horror film in which the monster is systemic racism. When I turn on the news or get bombarded by the daily series of presidential tweets, I feel that I'm living in my own personal horror film, only the monster here is systemic xenophobia.

*Get out.*

That's how I feel as the weather turns cold and snow starts to cascade down almost every day.

I need a break.

I need some time off.

I need some time away.

Then, as if in answer to my prayer, I receive a call from the medical clinic at the US military base at Camp As Sayliyah, in Qatar — the same one I applied to a year ago, when I considered leaving Dawson.

"The guy we hired just bailed on us," the clinic's business manager, Kyle, says. "We're desperate. We need somebody fast. You wouldn't be interested, would you?"

"Permanently? I don't think I could —"

"No, only for one month while we fill the position."

*This is exactly what I need,* I think. *It's a good cause. I'll be serving our troops, and I can get out of Dawson for enough time to catch my breath.*

"This is perfect," I say. "I'll do it."

"You're saving my life," Kyle says.

"Actually," I say, "you're saving mine."

I tell Musarrat of the offer, we work out the logistics of my month away, and then I sit down with Stacey.

"I'm sorry to do this," I say. "I'm just feeling overwhelmed again. I need a little break."

Stacey laughs. "You call working on an army base a break?"

I laugh along with her and then explain that I really would like to spend some time in a Muslim country where I can go to a mosque to pray and where people won't stare at me or look at me differently, where I won't stick out. I also wonder — I hope — that if our troops see me, a Muslim

237

physician, taking time away from my regular position to help them, that this might make a positive impression.

"I think the troops will absolutely see that," Stacey says.

I slowly shake my head.

"Man," I say, "the things I do to prove I'm not a terrorist."

I travel to Dubai and other Arab countries routinely and without difficulty, so I'm not prepared for the enormous amount of red tape I run into to get security clearances to leave for Qatar.

Leaving requires an inordinate amount of credentials, including submitting to a background check and obtaining a copy of my fingerprints that must be kept with me at all times on something called a fingerprint card. When the process seems to be dragging on, I call our local sheriff's office.

"Yeah, hi, I need to get a fingerprint card. Is this something you can do?"

"Yeah, just come over and we'll take care of you," the guy who answers the phone says. "Give me your name, and I'll look out for you."

"Dr. Ayaz Virji."

"What do you need a fingerprint card for?"

"I'm going on a mission trip to serve our troops overseas," I say.

"Dr. Ayaz Virji," the guy repeats, emphasizing my last name, seeming to mull it over. "I know the name. Dawson, right? I've heard of you."

I hold my breath. Then I immediately go to my dark place.

*This is why I'm leaving,* I think. *I need a break from this crap. From people stereotyping me just because of my name, because I'm a Muslim, because he's heard about my lectures.*

"Right," I say, trying to squelch the hostility I feel tickling my throat. "Dr. Ayaz Virji, from Dawson. That's me."

"That's what I thought. Dr. Virji, as a vet, I want to thank you for your service."

Now I'm shut down. I have stereotyped *him.* I feel humbled and slightly ashamed.

Yep.

I need to get away.

I need to clear my head.

"Well, I should be the one thanking you," I say to the man.

*I need a break.*


I do everything I'm supposed to do way ahead of time, but the security clearance process drags on . . . and on . . . and on.

The day before I'm scheduled to leave for Qatar, I have not received my final clearance. I call the clinic, I call the sheriff, I call everyone I can think of to try to put a rush on my clearance. Finally, I get word that my clearance will take at least one more week. The reason? The Trump administration's Department of Homeland Security simply does not employ enough personnel to process the number of security clearances on their desks. I explain the delay to the clinic's manager, who understands but says there's nothing he can do, and then I call Stacey, who tells me the doctor they've arranged to cover for me for the month has already started. I'm suddenly a man without a destination, a job, or a plan for one entire month.

My security clearance finally comes through — at the end of the month. It's too late. The troop medical clinic has had to go without a doctor for that whole time. Since I have been replaced in Dawson, with no other place to be, I decide to take the family on a spontaneous vacation to Dubai.

I come back feeling recharged. In February, I go back to work at the clinic, attend to bariatric patients, and resume the lectures. I also begin to contemplate my future. Though the Body Togs weight loss business continues to boom, my contract at the hospital expires in June. Stacey initiates a preliminary conversation about my signing a new long-term agreement.

Then, in late March, hate comes to Dawson.

I get word that a group in Montevideo, the town where people confronted me and called me the anti-Christ before and after my lecture, has invited a Christian pastor and former Muslim to denounce Islam. I learn that the group has purposely booked this guy to counter me. They want to hear the "other side."

I look up the guy online. Among other bogus pronouncements, he "disputes that Islam is an Abrahamic faith." In his talk, he says, he will contrast the "True Jesus of the Bible with the false Jesus of Islam." He doesn't come from a place of real scholarship or present a measured voice of disagreement. He's known for delivering a three-hour screed, a bigoted, hysterical diatribe of hatred, a vicious attack on my religion. Pastor Mandy talks to a few people in Montevideo, confirming what we've both believed: that he has been invited to speak as a direct response against me. He's delivering an antidote to my lecture. This saddens and sickens me.

A thought — a simple four-word question — begins to thrum through my head, unsettling me.

*What will it take?*

What will it take for me to finally say, "Enough?"

What will it take for me to give up my practice and the lectures and leave?

I've stayed through the election of Donald Trump, his proposed travel ban, the suggestion of a Muslim registry, discovering a swastika in front of my house, people calling me the anti-Christ, people sending me hate mail and death threats, hearing about bacon smeared on my friend's windshield. And now this — the welcoming of a speaker in the next town who will spew venom and lies about my religion.

*What will it take?*

Pastor Mandy, as incensed as I am, talks with some people in Montevideo about hosting a "peace panel" at approximately the same time as the hate speaker's talk. They decide to invite representatives of many faiths and viewpoints, including me, a nun, a rabbi, a Native American, and perhaps even an atheist, all of us discussing inclusion, acceptance, and love. Someone suggests that after our panel, we should all march to the site of the hate speaker's talk and protest peacefully.

As the date of the hate speaker's talk draws closer, I wonder how many people will attend the event. Will the residents of Montevideo reject him or embrace him? Then I hear that the talk and the peace panel have generated media attention from local and perhaps even national news outlets.

The Montevideo government begins to worry about the potential for hostility, and maybe even violence. It abruptly cancels the peace panel and urges Pastor Mandy to reschedule for the following week. As it turns out, I will be out of town on business on the day of the hate speaker's talk. I hold off on deciding whether to attend the now rescheduled peace panel.

"I'm going to the guy's talk," our friend Austin, the aide at the high school, tells me.

"You don't have to do that," I say to him.

"No, I do. I want to hear him."

On the week of the talk in Montevideo, I pick up the *Dawson Sentinel* and see both an advertisement and an article announcing the event. Spread across three columns of the paper, the article lists in bullet points ten topics the speaker will cover, including "ways to equip the next generation to boldly defend their Christian faith." He attacks the concept of "interfaith dialogue," calling it a deception and arguing that such dialogue is "compromising the Gospel and our national security."

*How does he get away with this?* I wonder.

And then I feel a rush of anger as I realize that my hometown paper, the *Dawson Sentinel,* actually accepted and printed an advertisement and an outline of hate — over three columns.

*What will it take?*

"The number of people who actually attend this guy's talk," I tell a friend. "That's the key for me. If he gets a small turnout, then it's a blip on the radar screen, meaningless. I won't care. I'll chalk it up to a few people who really hate Muslims, hate me, or just morbid curiosity, and I'll forget about it and move on."

"What if he draws a big crowd?" my friend asks.

"I don't know," I say, closing my eyes and rubbing my temples. "I really don't know."

I spend the day of the hate speaker's talk at a medical convention in San Diego, promoting Body Togs. I left Dawson feeling optimistic that the medical community would support the weight loss program, especially the concept that wearable weights can actually work over time to help people shed pounds. I am completely unprepared for how enthusiastically the medical community embraces us. I leave the convention sky high, seeing that what I began as a side venture may be on the verge of really taking off.

My high lasts for about ten minutes. As I walk into my hotel room, Austin rings my cell to tell me about the talk in Montevideo.

"I just got back," he says.

"Well?"

"Worst three hours of my life," he says, sounding shaken.

"Oh, no. How many people showed up?"

He pauses. "Two hundred."

I spit the number back at him. *Two hundred?*"

"More or less. Maybe more."

"I can't believe it."

"I know," Austin says. "He got everybody worked up. He lies and says all these disgusting things about Muslims."

"Like what?"

Austin levels his voice. "Like all Muslims are going to Hell and they're trying to subvert the government. He told everyone that they should not be friends with Muslims."

245

I feel the anger coming, storming. I start to pace.

"I don't want to hear any more," I say.

"I'm staying over at your house tonight," Austin says. "I'm going to sleep downstairs in the living room."

I skid to a stop. "Why?"

"He got people riled up. You're not home until tomorrow. I —" He holds for a moment, then says, "Just a precaution."

"You really think you have to stay at my house?"

"It'll make me feel better," he says.

"Okay," I say. "Thank you, Austin. I'll be home tomorrow evening."

"A precaution," he repeats. "That's all. Don't worry." Then after a long pause, he mumbles again, "The worst three hours of my life."

As I drive through the rolling Minnesota farmland on my way home from the Minneapolis–St. Paul airport, I go through a frenzy of emotion. At first, I feel the anger rise. I can't bottle it up. But then the anger recedes to something more primal and gut wrenching.

I need to protect my family.

We have plummeted into a new reality. I feel as if I've fallen into a pit and am hurtling toward the bottom — only I have no sense of where the bottom may be.

How can a pastor — in the name of Christianity — espouse such venom, such hatred? Pastor Mandy must feel so offended, so outraged.

*I feel outraged.*

And then I feel numb.

Stacey and I have begun talking about my next contract. But this last incident makes me wonder if I have come to the end.

*What will it take?*

Three hours later, I pull up in front of our house, close my eyes, breathe, gather myself, and walk into a house humming with life, with energy, with no trace of fear or worry. Austin greets me. He looks exhausted but calm, glad to see me. He spent a fitful, watchful night. He saw or heard nothing out of the ordinary.

"Thanks again for staying here, Austin," I say. "I'm sorry you had to go through that."

"It's okay. I don't understand how someone can lie like that in the name of Christianity. Everything he said was the opposite of Christianity."

"I don't know, Austin."

Then Austin's voice rises into an appeal. "If you go anywhere, take me with you."

The day after the talk, I hear that several Somali families — Muslims — living in Wilmer, a nearby town, have received death threats.

I take that personally. Those folks have done nothing except be dark-skinned and Muslim. I think about the ad and article that appeared in the *Dawson Sentinel,* and I go ballistic. I speed walk over to the office of the *Sentinel* and ask to see the editor. His assistant, a man I'll call Cliff, tells me that he has gone for the day.

"Okay," I say, exhaling slowly. "Then I will tell you. Please pass on what I'm about to say. I am personally offended by what you did, putting that ad in the paper. Maybe it was a business decision, but let me ask you this: How much does it cost to get a new doctor in town?"

I stare at Cliff. His eyes begin to flutter. He looks away.

"Cliff," I say, regaining his attention. "This guy has a message of hate. Ours is a message of love. And please don't give me the free speech argument. There is no equivalency here."

"Okay," Cliff says, eyeing the door longingly. I half expect him to leap up from his desk and make a run for it.

"You will no longer get any Body Togs advertising or Body Togs business," I say to him, my voice lifting. "I'm talking about ads, printing, all of it. You can close my account."

Cliff squirms in his chair, rakes his fingers through his hair. I've hit a nerve.

"Well, hold on there, Dr. Ayaz —"

"Cliff, when I first moved to Dawson, I gave you all of our printing, our business cards, all of our advertising. Everyone said, 'They're more expensive than other places.' I said, 'I don't care. I want to support local.' Now I'm done. I don't have to support you anymore. You've lost me. You have lost all my business."

Cliff knocks on his desk as if it's a door, then starts to reach for his phone. "Maybe, you know, I should call —"

I stop him short. I want Cliff and the editor of the paper to share a tiny portion of my hurt. I want them to feel — something.

"I also told my wife that I prefer she not advertise with you anymore," I say matter-of-factly, without anger. "She's a good customer. I really don't know what she's going to do. Contrary to popular belief, Muslim men do not control Muslim

249

women. She will make her own decision."

"Okay, see, right there, I really need to call, you know, I mean, I wish you wouldn't —"

"Good-bye, Cliff," I say, and storm out of the office.

Over dinner that night, Doug, normally low-key and measured, starts railing about our local radio station.

"They pushed that event very heavily," he says. "It was all over that radio station."

"Really? The station manager's a good guy. He's offered to take Faisal deer hunting with a bow and arrow many times. How can he not see this? I want to talk to him."

Doug takes his phone out of his pocket, punches in some numbers, then springs out of his chair, nods at his phone, and hands it to me.

"Here you go," he says.

"Hey, this is Dr. Virji," I say into the phone. "I want to talk to you about the ads you broadcast on your station about that speaker in Montevideo. You know who I mean."

"Yeah, I believe I know who you mean," the station manager says.

"I thought you might." I pause, and then I say, "I just want you to know that your ads personally offend me. I don't know what you were thinking, but this guy embodies hate. He insults me. He tells people not to be friends with Muslims and that I'm trying to subvert the government. You helped him make his event successful. I don't know how you explain that."

After a long pause, the station manager says, "This is free speech. I've got federal regulations. I can't deny him."

"Okay," I say. "Then I want to advertise the KKK on your radio. I want to advertise the good side of white supremacy. Will you put that on your radio?"

"Of course not."

"What's the difference?"

"You didn't hear the ad," the station manager says. "The ad was benign."

Man, this guy doesn't get it. I hear my voice rise. "So you whitewashed somebody's hate, and now you're willing to defend it."

"Dr. Virji, you're taking this out of proportion." He holds and says in what I hear is a twinge of regret, "I didn't feel good about the ad."

"Then why did you do it?"

"I had to because of federal regulations."

"If I want to have a terrorist group advertise on your radio station, is that free speech?"

A pause. I can almost hear him thinking this over.

"No," he says finally. "It's not the same thing."

"There are limits to free speech, and you know it," I say. "I would argue that advertising this guy's talk ultimately incited hatred and did constitute a danger. People received *death threats* because of him."

Silence. Nothing.

He knows I'm right.

"Okay, so, listen, since you say you're in a bind, that there's nothing you can do, that's fine. Just take this phone call as a public complaint from one of your consumers about what you did, and that's it."

"I don't want to leave it like that," the station manager says practically in a whimper.

"You said there's nothing you can do, and I said fine."

A long silence follows.

"So that's it," I say. "I'm not hanging up on you, but I am hanging up."

*Get out.*

I sit across from Stacey in her office. A new, unsigned contract rests on her desk between us. I look at her, and simultaneously we shake our heads. She manages a thin smile.

"We've been here before," she says. "Unfortunately."

"Last place I wanted to be," I say. I rake my fingers through my hair. "For over a year now I've been feeling either incredibly tense or irrationally angry. This is not who I am."

"I know," Stacey says.

"I don't want to live in this emotional place. It's exhausting."

"Nobody would."

I absently tap the top page of the contract and shake my head again. "Every time I feel that it's the minority, that it's just a small percentage — I can handle that." I wave toward the window, gesturing vaguely in the direction of where I imagine Montevideo lies. "Then this kind of crap happens. People get death threats. This guy gets welcomed. And now, did you hear, he's coming back?"

"What?"

"Yeah. They invited him *back.* For another talk. Part two. Hate speaker two point oh. I guess he didn't get a chance to spew enough hatred. He only spoke for three hours."

Stacey sighs and straightens her already erect posture. "Well, that just makes me feel, I don't know —"

"Angry?" I say.

"Yes," she says. "And sad."

"Welcome to Donald Trump's America," I say. "Welcome to my world."

A well-meaning group of people representing all faiths want to discuss the speaker, what his talk meant, and how they feel about it. They hold an event in Montevideo, but I don't attend. I'm on call, and I don't want to explore my feelings any further. I don't want to give this guy one more second of my time or my attention. He is exactly what extremists want. They want people like the residents of Montevideo to hate us and to fear us. They want to turn the world against us. I don't want to acknowledge that he is having any impact at all. Yet the town invited him back.

A day or so after the event in Montevideo, Musarrat goes on a lunch date with a couple of her female friends. As I expected, they discuss the Montevideo speaker. One woman, Nancy, who is Caucasian, attended the talk and plans to attend the interfaith discussion.

"I don't understand something," she says to Musarrat. "Why do so many immigrants want to come here in the first place?"

"What did you tell her?" I ask Musarrat. We are standing side by side at the kitchen sink. She washes dishes, I dry.

"I gave her a very politically correct answer," Musarrat says. "I don't want to make waves. I don't see the point in that. We do have to live here."

"Yeah, well, I would have said, 'You're right. Why are *you* here, Nancy? Your ancestors are Norwegian. You're an immigrant. Why don't you go back to Norway? Unless you're Native American, you should just leave.' I can just hear her. 'But I'm *white.*' "

"You're right," Musarrat says, eyeing me as if I've gone out of my mind. "*That's* what I should've said."

"I am so over this," I say. "People come to this country for our alleged values and our freedom and our institutions of learning and our opportunities. We are supposed to be that city on the hill. We are not supposed to discriminate. We are supposed to be that light."

I pause and look down at the still wet water glass in my hand.

"This past year," I say, "that light has gone out."

I retreat. I find myself not wanting to go out and be part of the community. I avoid Wanda's Diner, the bowling alley, the Rusty Duck, the pharmacy. I stick to the hospital, working with Doug on Body Togs, and

255

hanging with my family. When I do walk into town, I hear and feel a low-level hum. People are still talking about the hate speaker. I hear comments that run the gamut from people feeling outraged to others feeling as if they've learned something, the extremely negative to the very positive. I decide to take Pastor Mandy's advice when she calls one night.

"You have a high profile in the community," she says.

"Oh, I don't know —"

"You do. You know you do. You're the *doctor.* Everyone knows you."

"All right," I reluctantly admit.

"You need to keep quiet for a little while. If you can."

"I can do that. I will do that. I'll just chill out."

In my peripheral vision, I catch a look from Musarrat. She raises an eyebrow.

*You? Chill out?*

I keep a low profile for a week or so. When I do interact with folks in town, I sense them assessing me, gauging how I feel. Maybe it's my imagination.

But I do know from what Pastor Mandy and Doug have told me that some people in the community have said, "Oh, he just likes to complain," or "He whines when some-body says something negative."

Time saves me — in this case, ten days' distance from the event — saves me or at least calms me down. Time and work. Work fulfills me, distracts me, and serves as my therapy. Of course, there are certain moments when I find myself agonizing over the extreme disconnects I experience, challenging my reality. I see on the news and read news stories that show how Donald Trump somehow manages to come across as both a bully and a victim — at the same time. It's inconceivable and contradictory, yet he pulls it off, at least to a huge portion of American people. He succeeds because so many people appear afraid of him while so many others defend him. People *here*. In Dawson. They actually defend the bully.

I cannot fathom this absurdity.

Yet I see how people defend the hate speaker and I wonder — *did he bring out the evil in them?*

*Or was it there already?*

I ask myself, I ask Musarrat, I ask Mandy, I ask Stacey, I ask Jason: How do you explain this sea change in America? Is it permeating from the top down? Or did the bottom finally elect its own value system?

Amid all of this, I hear a story that frightens me at first and then, strangely, gives me hope.

During the question-and-answer portion of the hate speaker's talk, a prominent man in the area, a farmer, a Jewish guy, rises to ask a question. He chooses his words carefully. Given the atmosphere, he doesn't want to say anything too provocative. But he does want to challenge the speaker's premise — that Muslims want to overthrow the government and that Islam came from the Devil.

The Jewish man asks his question, and the speaker tells him that he is not welcome at the event. He tells the farmer to leave. The crowd, in support of the speaker, erupts — and turns on the Jewish guy. A few men go at him. Someone puts his hands on him, shoves him. A police officer at the scene intervenes and escorts the farmer safely from the room, the crowd jeering, shouting, cursing, booing at his back.

When they get outside, the farmer, who is shaking, thanks the police officer for stepping in. The officer says he was just doing his job, but he, too, was glad to get out of that room. And then the police officer tells the farmer that he is Muslim.

What are the odds?

A Muslim police officer and a Jewish farmer share a spiritual connection at a lecture filled with hatred and lies about Islam.

Yes. That story gives me hope.

I know this to be true from the very depths of my being.

Embracing hate is not okay, and neither is accommodating it. I should not have to explain that. These two lectures — mine and the hate speaker's — are not equal.

One is "Love Thy Neighbor," the other is "Hate Thy Neighbor." Yet, somehow, both messages are treated equally by the community, by the country, and they shouldn't be.

I take a deep breath and ask myself — again — *If not me, then who?*

I commit to continuing the lectures and accept all that comes with that commitment. I smile to myself ironically. *You think you've had some challenges, and then a whole other level of challenges comes at you.*

It hits my core. I sometimes feel as if I'm getting pounded even harder. The speaker has come back to Montevideo for a second time. How can that be? Aren't three hours of hatred enough? Apparently not. The people around me keep falling for this crap.

I have to keep doing the lectures. I know

that now. It has become a mission, not my only purpose but *a* purpose. I fight through the challenges. I accept them. Mainly, it challenges love as a verb. That alone is becoming harder to do. Love is difficult to do. It's hard. Love is hard.

I didn't come to Dawson to talk about my faith. If I had known my faith would need defending here, I wouldn't have come. None of this was part of the deal.

I keep going. I work at the free clinic. I find that work important, difficult, but it reminds me of all that we have and take for granted. Health. The means to seek care when we need it. We have to help those who need help. Sometimes these folks have no other place to turn. Sometimes they just don't know how to ask.

I keep a lid on my emotions. That, too, is hard. Some days I feel like I'm on an emotional roller coaster. Prayer helps. My family helps. My friends help. And seeing patients helps. It grounds me. Balances me. Gives me hope. Today I will see patients in my bariatric clinic, patients whom I admire so much. They are struggling to survive, but they are committed to the hard work of a healthier life. Though I know I am helping them, what they don't know is that they are helping me. They're doing something real.

They inspire me.

One afternoon, I meet with Stacey. We talk about the clinic, the hospital expansion, the new state-of-the-art equipment we want to purchase. We talk about Dawson. We talk about the basic goodness and kindness of the people here. We talk about how hard I can sometimes be on people around me, but mostly on myself. We talk about the future. We talk about hope. Yes. We talk about hope.

And then I grab a pen and sign my new contract.

# POSTSCRIPT

Dr. Virji and Pastor Mandy continue their Love Thy Neighbor lecture series in churches, schools, and community centers in the Midwest. Since release of this book, Dr. Virji has accepted a Health and Wellness Directorship at New York University in Abu Dhabi, UAE. He continues seeing patients at Johnson Memorial Health Services on a part-time basis and maintains his permanent residence in Dawson, Minnesota. He remains devoted to educating people about his faith and extending a message of love, inclusion, and acceptance to communities like Dawson across our great country.

# ACKNOWLEDGMENTS

**From Ayaz Virji:**
In the name of God, the beneficent, the merciful. Thanks to all those who contributed to the realization of this work. Without the support of so many, neither the "Love Thy Neighbor" lecture series nor this book could have happened.

Thanks to Alan for his writing brilliance. Thanks to Derek Reed and Anthony Mattero for their guidance through the publication process. Special thanks to Pastor Mandy France for being such a strong voice of social justice and inspiration to me. Thanks to Stacey Lee, whose optimism and positive attitude helped me through challenging times. Thanks to Doug Peterson, Austin Ireland, and Jason Connover for your friendship. My family is so blessed to have you in our lives.

Thank you to my mentors at Georgetown University, Dean Ray Mitchell, Dr. Carolyn

Robinowitz, Dr. Robert Cutillo, Professor John Voll, and many others — too many to mention. I think of you often.

Finally, and saving the best for last, thank you to Musarrat, my beautiful wife and rock! I am so blessed to have you as my soulmate.

**From Alan Eisenstock:**
Working with Dr. Ayaz Virji, I was privileged to observe firsthand a force of nature. Ayaz, you roar through your days, a whirlwind, expressing deep compassion to every human being you encounter, displaying uncompromising moral and ethical conviction in every situation, and an unwavering love of family, friends, colleagues, neighbors, and strangers. It is a blessing to know you and work with you. It is a gift to call you my friend.

The first notion that there might be a book here happened over lunch with my agent, Anthony Mattero. He mentioned that his assistant, Alex Rice, had read an article about Dr. Ayaz Virji featured on the front page of the *Washington Post*. Alex, excellent work, and thank you. Anthony, my brother-in-arms and co-conspirator, found the perfect home in Convergent at Penguin Random House, and the ideal editor in

266

Derek Reed. Anthony, I can never find the words to thank you and tell you how much I appreciate you being at my side, every day.

Derek, you saw this book from the beginning and your vision stayed clear. Thank you for your exquisite editing, patience, and commitment. I consider myself fortunate to be working with the absolute dream team of Ayaz, Anthony, and Derek. And thanks to everyone at Convergent who from cover to design have produced a beautiful book.

I'm grateful to the folks I met in Dawson who were welcoming, warm, and open. I especially thank Pastor Mandy France, Doug Peterson, Jason Connover, Stacey Lee, Wanda Gannon Coon, and, of course, Musarrat for spending hours with me and patiently answering all my questions. I thank the entire Virji family — Musarrat, Ayaz, Faisal, Imran, and Maya — for being such gracious hosts.

Thanks to my supportive friends and family: David Ritz, Madeline and Phil Schwarzman, Susan Pomerantz and George Weinberger, Susan Baskin and Richard Gerwirtz, Kathy Montgomery and Jeff Chester, Linda Nussbaum, Larry Ross, Gary Meisel, Ed Feinstein, Jim Eisenstock, Jay Eisenstock, Loretta Barrabee, Lorraine, Linda, Diane, Alan, Chris, Ben, and Nate.

# ABOUT THE AUTHOR

**Ayaz Virji** is a family physician practicing in Dawson, Minnesota. He received his B.A. in history at Georgetown University in 1996 and his M.D. from Georgetown Medical School in 2000. In addition to his 14 years of medical practice, Dr. Virji has authored several peer-reviewed scientific publications, and one patent, and he studies comparative religion in his free time. He continues to present his "Love Thy Neighbor" lectures in schools, libraries, community centers, places of worship, colleges, and universities throughout the country.